CAMPAIGN • 238

ST MIHIEL 1918

The American Expeditionary Forces' trial by fire

DAVID BONK

ILLUSTRATED BY HOWARD GERRARD

Series editor Marcus Cowper

First published in 2011 by Osprey Publishing
Midland House, West Way, Botley, Oxford OX2 0PH, UK
44-02 23rd St, Suite 219, Long Island City, NY 11101, USA

E-mail: info@ospreypublishing.com

Print ISBN: 978 1 84908 391 1
PDF e-book ISBN: 978 1 84908 392 8
EPUB e-book ISBN: 978 1 84908 880 0

Editorial by Ilios Publishing Ltd, Oxford, UK (www.iliospublishing.com)
Design: The Black Spot
Index by Sandra Shotter
Originated by Blenheim Colour Ltd, Eynsham, Oxford
Cartography: Boundford.com
Bird's-eye view artworks: The Black Spot
Printed in China through Worldprint ltd.

11 12 13 14 15 10 9 8 7 6 5 4 3 2 1

A CIP catalog record for this book is available from the British Library.

EDITOR'S NOTE

All photographs in this book are from the US National Archives.

ARTIST'S NOTE

Readers may care to note that the original paintings from which the color plates in this book were prepared are available for private sale. The Publishers retain all reproduction copyright whatsoever. All inquiries should be addressed to:

Howard Gerrard, 11 Oaks Road, Tenterden, TN30 6RD, UK

The Publishers regret that they can enter into no correspondence upon this matter.

MEASUREMENT CONVERSIONS

Imperial measurements are used almost exclusively throughout this book. The exception is weapon calibers, which are given in their official designation, whether metric or imperial. The following data will help in converting the imperial measurements to metric.

1 mile = 1.6km	1lb = 0.45kg
1oz = 28g	1 yard = 0.9m
1ft = 0.3m	1in. = 2.54cm/25.4mm
1 gal = 4.5 liters	1pt = 0.47 liters
1 ton (US) = 0.9 tonnes	1hp = 0.745kW

THE WOODLAND TRUST

Osprey Publishing are supporting the Woodland Trust, the UK's leading woodland conservation charity, by funding the dedication of trees.

Key to military symbols

XXXXX Army Group	XXXX Army	XXX Corps	XX Division	X Brigade	III Regiment	II Battalion
I Company/Battery	••• Platoon	•• Section	• Squad	Infantry	Artillery	Cavalry
Airborne	Unit HQ	Air defense	Air Force	Air mobile	Air transportable	Amphibious
Antitank	Armor	Air aviation	Bridging	Engineer	Headquarters	Maintenance
Medical	Missile	Mountain	Navy	Nuclear, biological, chemical	Ordnance	Parachute
Reconnaissance	Signal	Supply	Transport movement	Rocket artillery	Air defense artillery	

Key to unit identification

Unit identifier — Parent unit

Commander

(+) with added elements
(−) less elements

CONTENTS

Strategic overview of the St Mihiel salient

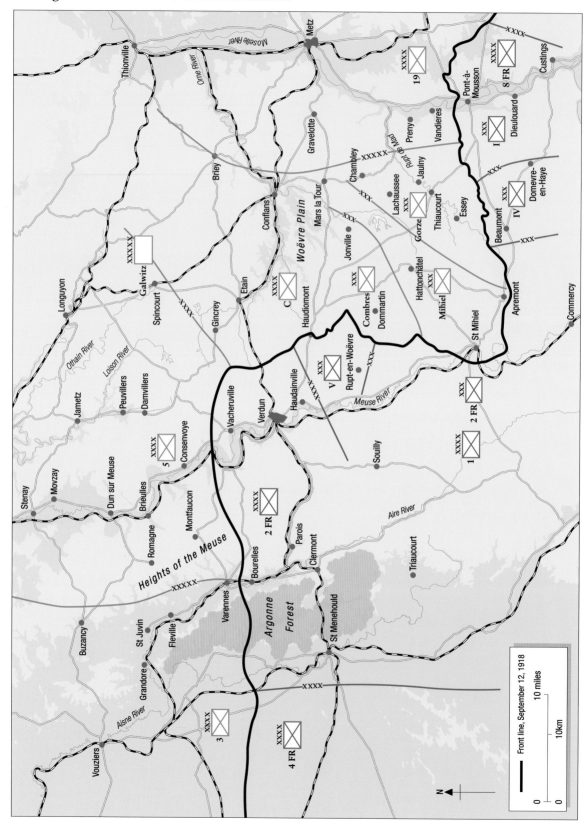

ORIGINS OF THE CAMPAIGN

In March 1918 the German Army launched a series of sledgehammer blows against both the British and French sectors of the Western Front, driving the British back toward the Channel ports and the French toward Paris. Operation *Michael* was the first in a series of German attacks launched over the next several months intended to shatter Allied morale and force the Allies to agree to a peace settlement before the full impact of expanding American manpower made victory impossible.

American Commander-in-Chief John J. Pershing found the Allied high command in disarray. Leaving a meeting with General Philippe Pétain on March 21, 1918, Pershing was surprised to learn that the situation along the British front was more serious than had been suggested. On March 25 Pershing met again with Pétain as rumors circulated that the French government had begun preliminary planning to abandon Paris for Bordeaux. Pétain admitted that he had ordered the headquarters moved to Chantilly and that Allied losses exceeded 150,000. More troubling was the impression that the French would not fulfill a previous mutual-aid agreement to assist the

Hindenburg (left) and Ludendorff (right) with Kaiser Wilhelm. Both generals hoped that the Spring Offensive would force the Allies to negotiate a peace before the full weight of American resources could be brought to bear.

British. Rather than maintaining connection with Sir Hubert Gough's British Fifth Army, which was staggering under German attacks, Pétain appeared to be deploying his reserves to protect the northern approaches to Paris.

In response to the crisis the French General Ferdinand Foch (made a Marshal of France on August 6) was appointed as overall Allied commander. On March 28, 1918, Pershing offered Foch the use of American troops. By spring 1918 the United States had almost 300,000 men deployed in various stages of training in France. Despite Pershing's desire to commit American troops, it wasn't until the end of April that the 1st Division relieved two French divisions at Montdidier. The 2nd, 26th, and 42nd divisions were completing their initial training and were then assigned to various sectors along the front. The 3rd, 5th, and 23rd divisions, intended to be organized as the American III Corps, were ordered to reinforce French divisions. Assigned to the British were the American 28th and 77th divisions.

On May 27, 1918, the same day as the Germans opened Operation *Blücher*, the 1st Division captured the village of Cantigny. In response to the new German offensive, Pershing assigned the 2nd Division to assist the French in stemming the German push toward Paris. The 2nd Division stopped the German advance on June 3 and over the next several weeks it fought a desperate battle to recapture Belleau Wood. Elements of the 3rd Division, although only partially trained, were assigned to French command and helped stop the German advance at Château-Thierry.

German commanders Quartermaster General Erich Ludendorff and Field Marshal Paul von Hindenburg, becoming increasingly concerned about the impact of the continuing influx of American troops, considered their next step. The objectives of Operation *Rheims* were to both draw Allied forces south from the Flanders front, where the Germans intended to throw a knockout blow against the British, and to isolate and capture the city of Rheims. The capture of Rheims would allow the Germans to use its rail facilities to support their troops in the Marne salient.

French intelligence identified the German plans as early as July 5, 1918, and by July 11 the French were sure of the date and objectives of the offensive. The final German offensive, Operation *Rheims*, began on July 15 and involved 24 front-line divisions supported by 17 in reserve. The American 3rd Division held the Marne River line at Château-Thierry against repeated German attacks, while the 26th, 28th, and 42nd divisions fought under the direction of French corps and army command. The German attacks failed to make substantial headway and the offensive was canceled on July 17.

Ludendorff recognized that the failure of his offensives to cripple the Allies represented a critical reversal. "The attempt to make the nations of the Entente inclined to peace before the arrival of the American reinforcements by means of German victories had failed. The energy of the army had not sufficed to deal the enemy a decisive blow before the Americans were on the spot in considerable force. It was quite clear to me that our general situation had thus become very serious."

The failure of Operation *Rheims* allowed the Allies to begin their counterattack against the Marne salient. On July 18 the American 1st and 2nd divisions, along with the First French Moroccan Division, attacked the heights south of Soissons. During this same period both the American 3rd and 4th divisions were deployed under French command. The American I Corps, commanded by Major-General Hunter Liggett, composed of the American 26th Division, later relieved by the 42nd Division and a French division, was engaged in support of the Soissons attack.

Between July 15 and August 6 American forces were fully engaged in the attack on the Marne salient. On August 18 General Pétain utilized the American 3rd Corps, composed of the 28th and 77th divisions, to open an offensive between Rheims and the Oise River. Several other American divisions were rotated into the line as part of the ongoing Allied offensives during the remainder of August.

Although the American units had played a pivotal role in stopping the German advance across the Marne River, their deployment had been haphazard and Pershing once again proposed concentrating American forces under a single command as part of an independent American army.

CHRONOLOGY

1917

April 6
The US Congress declares war on Germany.

June 13
General John J. Pershing and staff leave London for France.

June 26
American 1st Division and 5th Marine Regiment land in France.

September–December
American 2nd, 26th, and 42nd divisions complete deployment to France.

1918

March 21
Germans begin Spring Offensive with Operation *Michael*.

April 20
German attack on American 26th Division at Seicheprey.

May 27
Germans launch Operation *Blücher* and drive French forces from Chemin des Dames.

May 28
American 1st Division attacks and captures village of Cantigny.

June 3
German drive to Paris stopped by 5th Marines at Les Mares Farm.

June 6–25
American 2nd Division captures Belleau Wood.

July 15–17
German Operation *Rheims* achieves minimal gains. American 3rd, 26th, 28th, and 42nd divisions engaged in stopping German offensive.

July 18 to August 6
French–American Aisne–Marne offensive. American 1st and 2nd divisions and French Moroccan Division spearhead assault near Soissons.

July 24
Allied conference at Bonbon finalizes American plan for offensive against St Mihiel salient.

August 10
Marshal Foch and General Pershing agree on the creation of an independent American army.

September 2
Pershing objects to Marshal Foch's proposal to limit scale of St Mihiel offensive to prepare for Meuse–Argonne attack. Pershing agrees to scale back St Mihiel attack.

September 12
First US Army attacks St Mihiel salient. Germans initiate withdrawal from salient.

September 13
American 1st and 26th divisions meet at Vigneulles, cutting off tip of St Mihiel salient.

September 14
St Mihiel offensive ends. Select American units begin phased withdrawal and transfer to Meuse–Argonne.

October 2–9
American 2nd and 36th divisions assist Fourth French Army in offensive between Rheims and Argonne. The 2nd Division captures Mont Blanc.

September 26 to November 11
First US Army participates in the Meuse–Argonne offensive.

OPPOSING COMMANDERS

ALLIED

John Joseph Pershing was a schoolteacher for several years before securing an appointment to West Point Military Academy in 1882 at the age of 22. After graduating in 1886 Pershing served with the 6th Cavalry Regiment on the American western frontier. Pershing taught military science at the University of Nebraska while earning a law degree. He served in Cuba with the 10th (Negro) Cavalry Regiment during the Spanish American War, winning a commendation for his actions at San Juan Hill. Pershing found early military success during three tours in the Philippines battling the Moro insurgents. He served as military attaché in Japan and studied the evolution of military tactics during the 1905 Russo-Japanese War.

In 1906 President Theodore Roosevelt promoted Pershing, now married to the daughter of a Republican senator, to brigadier-general, over the heads of 862 other officers. Pershing served as the Governor of Moro province in the Philippines before being selected in 1915 to command American forces pursuing Pancho Villa in Mexico. Although he was ultimately unsuccessful

Marshal Foch and Pershing enjoyed a cordial but strained relationship. While Pershing deferred to Foch in his role as Supreme Allied Commander he insisted that a separate American army be organized and allowed to conduct independent operations.

in capturing or killing Villa, his time in the southwest provided Pershing with experience overseeing an American expeditionary force dependent on extended supply lines. Pershing's role also impressed President Woodrow Wilson and Secretary of War Newton Baker. In particular, the President and Secretary credited Pershing for his strict adherence to their initial instructions, which were intended to limit American intervention in Mexico.

With America's declaration of war in April 1917, Pershing was appointed to command the American forces in Europe on May 24, 1917. Arriving in Europe on June 8, Pershing began the work of building an American army, work that would see its fulfillment with the St Mihiel offensive. Pershing engaged in bitter conflict with both British and French political and military leadership over the training and ultimate disposition of American forces during the remainder of 1917 and into 1918. He resisted demands that American forces be amalgamated into British and French units. Initially the proposed amalgamation was intended to be the most efficient way to train American forces, but the crisis created by the German Spring Offensive of 1918 caused the British to demand an infusion of American manpower to supplement their depleted units. Pershing resisted intense pressure from the British and French for a change in American policy but modified the deployment program to respond to the crisis in the spring and early summer of 1918.

In response to Marshal Foch's reversal of policy in late August 1918, Pershing committed the newly formed First US Army to a series of operations in the Meuse–Argonne that they were inadequately prepared to undertake. Although the St Mihiel offensive captured over 15,000 Germans and drove them from the salient it failed to trap the vast majority of them, and by agreeing to limit the scope of the offensive Pershing may have missed achieving a strategic coup in capturing Metz and the Briey Iron Basin.

George S. Patton was born on November 11, 1885, into a family with a strong military tradition. Patton's ancestors had fought in the American Revolution, the Mexican War, and the American Civil War. Patton graduated from West Point in 1909 and joined the 15th Cavalry Regiment. An expert swordsman, Patton became the first Master of the Sword at the Mounted Service School in Fort Riley, Kansas. Patton commanded cavalry patrols along the Mexican border and joined Pershing on his expedition against Pancho Villa.

While serving on Pershing's staff in France, Captain Patton requested appointment to the newly organized United States Tank Corps in October 1917. In November 1917 he became head of the American Expeditionary Force Light Tank School at Langres. Patton, who had no prior knowledge of tanks, quickly acquainted himself with both the British Mark VI and French Renault tanks. After spending two weeks visiting French and British training camps, driving tanks, and visiting the Renault manufacturing plants, Patton and 1st Lieutenant Elgin Braine submitted a policy paper proposing a structure for the organization of the American tank forces. Patton outlined a case for utilizing the French Renault tank, as well as proposing a system for supply, strategic transportation, recovery and salvage, and training. He also included a lengthy section on strategic and tactical deployment of tanks, based on his conversations with French and British counterparts.

Patton oversaw the development of the American Light Tank School at Bourg. By the end of March 1917 Patton had both men and tanks. While in command of the tank training program, inspired by the shoulder patch of the 82nd Division, Patton authorized the development of the armor symbol and special collar insignia.

In August 1918, with preparations for the St Mihiel offensive about to begin, Patton, now promoted to lieutenant-colonel, was given command of the 1st Tank Brigade, consisting of two light-tank battalions. Patton was to play a pivotal role in the deployment of tanks in support of the St Mihiel offensive.

George Marshall was born December 31, 1880, in Uniontown, Pennsylvania, and attended the Virginia Military Institute, graduating in 1901. He joined the US Army in 1902 and served in the Philippines, returning in 1906 to enter officer-training school at Fort Leavenworth, Kansas. After earning his commission Marshall returned to service in the Philippines. Returning to the United States in 1916, Marshall was assigned to the 1st Division as Head of Operations and dispatched to France in June 1917 with Pershing.

Marshall spent the next year preparing the 1st Division for its introduction to combat. Marshall was responsible for coordinating the training and supplies for the division and, later, operational plans for raids. In May 1918 he oversaw the preparation of plans for the 1st Division attack at Cantigny. In July 1918 Marshall was reassigned to the Operations Section of the General Staff of General Headquarters, and was immediately assigned to prepare plans for an offensive to reduce the St Mihiel salient.

Over the next month Marshall worked on plans in response to the shifting number of American and French divisions to be committed to the operations. On August 20, 1918, Marshall was reassigned as Assistant to the Chief of Staff for the First US Army and continued to refine the plans for the attack. With Marshal Foch's decision to limit the St Mihiel operation Marshall was required to both revise the plans for the attack and develop plans for the transfer of men and *matériel* to the Meuse–Argonne offensive.

Born in Tarbes, France, **Ferdinand Foch** attended the Jesuit College in St Etienne and joined the French Army in 1870, experiencing French defeat in the disastrous Franco-Prussian War. Foch entered the Ecole Polytechnique in 1871, was commissioned as a lieutenant in 1873, and entered the Staff College as a captain in 1885. Appointed as an instructor in 1895, Foch led a reappraisal of the French defeat in 1870 and a reappreciation of examining military history as a means of refining military doctrine. Foch spent the next

LEFT
Lieutenant-Colonel Patton was a key member of the newly created American Tank Corps and was responsible for the its early organization and training.

RIGHT
Lieutenant-Colonel George Marshall (right) with General Pershing. Marshall was elevated to the planning section of the First US Army and was responsible for developing a series of offensive plans for St Mihiel and the logistical planning for transitioning American forces for the Meuse–Argonne attack.

15 years rising in rank and alternating between field command and positions at the Staff College. At the outbreak of World War I Foch was a lieutenant-general in command of the French XX Corps.

The crisis of March 1918, when French and British armies were pressed to their breaking point by successive German attacks, resulted in Foch being elevated to Supreme Commander. As Supreme Commander, he was responsible for coordinating Allied strategy and allocating resources. Foch was made Marshal of France on August 6, 1918.

In August 1918, Foch reversed course after approving the creation of the First US Army and sanctioning the St Mihiel offensive. At the urging of British Field Marshal Douglas Haig, Foch adopted an overall strategic plan that required the First US Army to be deployed in the Meuse–Argonne in time to begin attacks in late September 1918. He also limited the scope of the St Mihiel offensive. The combination of revised objectives and reduced timetables put an immense strain on the American forces involved in the St Mihiel offensive.

GERMAN

Max von Gallwitz was born in Breslau, Germany, in 1852. He joined the Army in 1870 and served as an artillery officer in the Franco-Prussian War. In an army dominated by aristocrats and predominantly Protestant, Gallwitz, a commoner and a Catholic, was able to rise to the rank of colonel and became Chief of Artillery in the War Ministry. He became a major-general in 1902 and was promoted to general and and appointed as inspector of field artillery by 1911. In 1913 Kaiser Wilhelm elevated him into the ranks of the Prussian nobility.

Transferred back to the Western Front in late 1915, Gallwitz commanded in the Verdun and Somme sectors. Considering Gallwitz one of his best officers, Ludendorff assigned him to command the Metz region in 1916. After the failed Spring Offensive, Gallwitz was assigned to defend the Meuse–Moselle sector. In overall command of the St Mihiel salient, Gallwitz responded with acerbity to the American attack, correctly identifying the focus of the attack and rushing reserves forward to buttress the Michel Stellung and protect Metz. Gallwitz was confused by American inaction after the initial attack, convinced that the ultimate American objective was Metz.

After the defeat in the St Mihiel salient, Gallwitz again confronted Pershing and the First US Army in the Meuse–Argonne. Gallwitz took advantage of the difficult terrain and the inexperience of the First US Army, stalling the initial American drive with masterful use of his limited reserves. A renewed American effort in early October slowly wore down German resistance and contributed to the German surrender on November 11, 1918.

Erich Ludendorff was born in Kruszewnia, Posen, in April 1865. He was commissioned as a lieutenant in 1885 after graduating from the Cadet School at Plon. In 1893 he was selected for the War Academy and recommended for appointment to the General Staff. Ludendorff was made a colonel in 1911 and then a major-general in 1914. Between 1904 and 1913 Ludendorff served as a staff officer and was appointed Chief of Staff in East Prussia at the outbreak of the war. In combination with Hindenburg, Ludendorff won decisive victories at Tannenberg (1914) and Masurian Lakes (1915). In 1916 Ludendorff was appointed quartermaster general. In continued partnership with Hindenburg, Ludendorff pressured Kaiser Wilhelm to dismiss officers who supported a negotiated peace settlement. Ludendorff was the mastermind of the German offensives of early 1918, which resulted in the elevation of Ferdinand Foch to Supreme Allied Commander. In July 1918 Ludendorff took effective control of all aspects of the German war effort. With the withdrawal of Russia from the war, Ludendorff conceived the Spring Offensive, which was intended to win the war before the Americans could tip the balance. The failure of the Spring Offensive to defeat the Allies resulted in the exhaustion of German offensive capabilities. By the time of the St Mihiel offensive Ludendorff suffered from both mental and physical exhaustion. He would later describe the news of the American offensive as "the worst days of my life."

OPPOSING ARMIES

An American doughboy in full combat gear. By the time of the St Mihiel offensive American infantry had adopted a variety of clothing adapted to the rigor of combat. In addition, heavy rains resulted in American troops wearing trenchcoats during the initial phase of the attack.

AMERICAN

First US Army

By the end of August 1918 American units in France had been blooded in a series of hard-fought engagements that highlighted the strengths and exposed the weaknesses of the American infantry. Although they had triumphed at Belleau Wood, Château-Thierry, along the Vesle River, and at Soissons, the cost in manpower had been high.

German opinion of their American opponents expressed high regard for their "morale, courage, and physique" but was dismissive of their "clumsy" tactics. Both German intelligence estimates and Pershing's headquarters staff noted a general failure to combine fire and movement. In training with tanks prior to the assault on Cantigny in May 1918, the French advisers emphasized the need for short rushes from shellhole to shellhole and were frustrated that the Americans were reluctant to take advantage of available cover.

After the early battles of June and July 1918, Pershing and his commanders understood the tactical shortcomings of even the most veteran of their units and sought to utilize the relative lull in combat to correct the most glaring problems. On August 5 a detailed directive was released to corps and division commanders outlining the expectations for training. The instructions specifically highlighted the need for small-unit training and emphasized that "platoon, company, and battalion commanders adopt no set formation for the attack in open fields but that each commander make the best possible use of the particular ground and of the various weapons at his disposal. Rushes of individuals or small units must be covered by fire; intelligent use of fire to cover movement enables ground to be gained at relatively small cost."

By August 1918 the quality of American divisions varied between blooded veterans and green, untested newcomers. The core of the American veteran divisions had fought in the late spring and summer at Belleau Wood, around Château-Thierry, and in the advance to the Vesle River. The 1st and 2nd divisions were joined by the 3rd, 4th, 26th, and 42nd divisions as first-rate units. The others, including the 89th and 5th divisions, had shown promise in limited roles, while the 82nd, 90th, and 91st divisions were largely untested.

The rapid expansion of the First US Army in 1917 and 1918 had resulted in the incorporation of immigrants from a multitude of countries. On September 9, 1918, as Pershing was preparing to commit the largest force of American troops since the American Civil War into combat, his headquarters

issued an order allowing alien soldiers serving in Europe to file for immediate citizenship without having to return to the United States.

United States Army Air Service

St Mihiel witnessed the commitment of massive air assets. The organization of American airpower in France began to take shape in January 1918 with the establishment of the 1st Pursuit and Training Center near Chalon in the Toul sector. The 95th Aero Squadron arrived in February, followed by the 136 men of the 94th Aero Squadron in early March 1918. The German offensive of March 21 forced the newly organized Americans to relocate to Epiez. The 94th Squadron, known as "Hat in the Ring," recorded its first kill on April 14 and was rejoined by the 95th in late April. Both squadrons and support staff relocated to Toul in early May and were joined by the 27th and 147th squadrons on June 1, as the 1st Pursuit Group. Throughout this period the Americans flew missions over the Toul–St Mihiel–Pont-à-Mousson front, sparring with the 64th and 65th *Jagdstaffeln* and various reconnaissance groups based at Mars-la-Tour, east of Metz.

At the same time as American pursuit squadrons were being organized, the 1st Observation Squadron began operations on April 11, 1918, flying patrols over the Seicheprey–Flirey area. By May 3 the 12th Squadron had joined the 1st, followed several weeks later by the 88th Aero Squadron, to form the I Corps Observation Group. In June the 90th and 99th squadrons also became active in the Toul sector.

The 96th Aero Squadron, trained for daylight bombing, arrived at Gondrecourt on May 18, 1918, and performed its first operational raid on June 12. Over the next six weeks the squadron struck at multiple targets, including rail facilities and ammunition dumps around Metz.

Although the American Air Force conducted its initial training in the Toul sector, the German offensives of June and July followed by Allied counterattacks resulted in reassignments to the Château-Thierry sector. The 1st Pursuit Group and I Corps Observation Group, joined by three balloon companies, gained invaluable experience and logged hundreds of hours over Belleau Wood, Fismes,

LEFT
American 95th Aero Squadron. Part of the 1st Pursuit Organization, the "Kicking Mules" flew their first combat mission in March 1918. Quentin Roosevelt, youngest son of President Teddy Roosevelt, was killed in action while flying with the 95th Aero Squadron, which ended the war with 65 confirmed kills.

RIGHT
Captain Eddie Rickenbacker after being awarded the Distinguished Service Cross. Rickenbacker, who was a well-known racecar driver before the war, was America's top ace in the war, credited with 26 enemy planes shot down.

LEFT
A Breguert bomber of the 96th Squadron. American flyers used a variety of French aircraft throughout the war.

RIGHT
American observation balloon. Balloons of this type were used extensively to gather intelligence on enemy dispositions. They were extremely vulnerable to enemy fighters and the two-man crews were equipped with parachutes.

and Soissons. The American airmen were blooded but they prepared to return to St Mihiel. While the veteran American air formations were over the Château-Thierry sector the 2nd Pursuit Group, which included the 13th and 139th aero squadrons, was being organized at Toul. They were joined by the 22nd and 49th squadrons. The 3rd Pursuit Group was also organized during this period and included the veteran 103rd Squadron, better known as the Lafayette Escadrille, and the 93rd, 28th, and 213th squadrons The 2nd and 3rd pursuit groups were joined by the newly created Day Bombardment Group composed of the 96th, 11th, and 20th squadrons. For the St Mihiel offensive the 1st Army Observation Group was composed of the 91st, 24th, and 9th squadrons.

Colonel William "Billy" Mitchell was promoted to command the First US Army Air Service in early August 1918, and on August 26 moved his headquarters to Ligny-en-Barrios to oversee the planning and implementation of coordinated air support for the St Mihiel offensive. By September 11, 1918, Mitchell commanded the largest collection of air units designated to participate in a single offensive during World War I. The American Air Service provided 12 pursuit, ten observation, one night observation, and three day-bombardment squadrons. Mitchell also had available the French Division Aérienne, 42 pursuit and day-bombardment squadrons, eight British night-bombardment squadrons, and several Italian air units. Mitchell would command a total of 1,481 aircraft operating out of 14 separate airfields.

AEF Tank Corps

On January 1, 1918, the American Tank Corps in France was commanded by Colonel Samuel Rockenbach. While the Army Air Service could rely on support from expatriate pilots serving with the French and British, the tank force was still in its infancy. Like the Army Air Service, Rockenbach had to rely on French and British equipment and support to establish training centers. Patton was assigned as Director of the Light Tank School, which was established at Bourg in January. By March, Patton had 10 tanks for training the two companies he had already established.

That same month, Rockenbach released a revised table of organization for the Tank Corps, designating five battalions of heavy tanks and 20 of light tanks, along with their associated headquarters and support organizations. The light-tank battalions would be numbered 1–40, and the heavy battalions 41–50. The 1st Light Tank Battalion was established on April 28, 1918. At Patton's direction a shoulder patch was designed by his staff, featuring a pyramid divided into red, yellow, and blue sections representing the firepower of artillery, the

maneuverability of the cavalry, and the ability to hold ground of the infantry. A second light-tank battalion was organized on June 6, 1918. During this period Patton, recently promoted to lieutenant-colonel, and his staff developed a unique American tactical doctrine, drawing from the experience of both the British and French. Heavy tanks would lead the assault, opening paths through the wire and across trenches and engaging enemy strongpoints. Light tanks, supported by the infantry, were expected to advance 100yds behind the heavy tanks and eliminate any remaining enemy concentrations. During this time the numbering protocol was also revised to designate the 1st and 2nd light-tank battalions as the 326th and 327th battalions.

GERMAN

German Army

Although the Germans had strengthened their defensive positions throughout the St Mihiel salient – adding bands of barbed wire, concrete reinforced strongpoints, and underground dugouts – the salient had long become a secondary front for the Germans, manned by units composed of depleted formations. Only eight understrength divisions, averaging about 5,000 men each, defended the perimeter. Two additional divisions were held in reserve. Of the front-line divisions only one of the eight was considered first class.

During the Spring Offensive the Germans had adopted a new offensive doctrine characterized by heavy artillery preparation and infiltration tactics. This new tactic achieved initial success and forced the Allies to adapt. The Allies had already been implementing a policy of defense in depth, which they perfected as a response to the last German offensive in late May 1918. The success of the Amiens attack on August 8, 1918, exposed the flaws of the German defensive deployment, catching front-line defenders by surprise and overwhelming them with artillery barrages. In response, German defensive doctrine shifted toward creating a deep outpost zone in advance of the main line of resistance and emphasizing improved intelligence-gathering to discern the enemy's plans.

American planners also recognized that German infantry formations had been allotted additional light machine guns, increasing their number to up to nine guns per company, to supplement their defensive firepower. German air strength in the salient included 213 aircraft, including approximately 84 combat aircraft, 105 reconnaissance aircraft, and 24 bombers.

LEFT
Patton (center) with members of his staff and tank crews during training. Patton recognized the combat potential of tanks and was responsible for the development of the initial organization of American tank battalions.

RIGHT
American tanks with crews. The tank on the right is equipped with a 7.92mm Hotchkiss machine gun while the tank on the left has a 37mm cannon in the turret.

On August 11, 1918, the German high command issued a reprimand to the Army, drawing conclusions from the defeat of the Second Army several days before. The communiqué admonished commanders to overcome the aversion of their troops to construct adequate fieldworks, particularly antitank defenses, noting that in the Somme some tanks were able to advance several miles and managed to overrun divisional headquarters. More directly, the unwillingness of troops to defend their positions to the last round was condemned. The directive also criticized the tendency for the front line to fall back if a small number of enemy units were able to bypass front-line strongpoints.

By the summer of 1918 German units varied greatly in their combat effectiveness and reflected the dwindling manpower pool available for replacements.

German dispositions

The German deployment in the salient included several defensive zones. The outpost sector was composed of the Wilhelm and Schroeter zones. The Wilhelm zone formed the majority of the forward area, and was 3–6 miles deep. The narrower Schroeter zone, named for the chief engineer of the German Crown Prince's army group, who laid out the defenses in 1917, and located at the rear of the Wilhelm zone, represented the last defensive line, protecting the interior area, which included Vigneulles and Doncourt. The Michel zone at the base of the salient included three separate defensive lines: the Hagen Stellung, Volker Stellung, and Kriemhild Stellung, all of which formed the Hindenburg Line.

Army Detachment C, under the command of Lieutenant-General Fuchs, held the salient. Army Detachment C was normally composed of 12 divisions organized into three corps. The western face was held by three divisions, known as the Combres Group, which included the 8th Landwehr Division, 13th Landwehr Division, and 35th Austro-Hungarian Regiment. The nose of the salient and a portion of the southern face was defended by the Mihiel Group, composed of the 5th Landwehr Division and the 192nd Saxon Division. The remainder of the southern face was defended by the 10th Division and 77th Reserve Division of the Gorze Group. To the east of the Gorze Group astride the Moselle River was the 255th Division of the 19th German Army. The 31st Division, 88th Division, 123rd Saxon Division, and 195th Division formed the army's reserve. Army Detachment C was part of Army Group Gallwitz, under overall command of General Max von Gallwitz.

As early as July 1918, Lt. Gen. Fuchs had expressed continued concern about the quality of the troops assigned to defend the salient. In the event that the salient needed to be evacuated, Fuchs demanded four assault divisions, two field-artillery regiments, ten battalions of heavy artillery, and substantial air reinforcements.

ORDERS OF BATTLE

AMERICAN

FIRST US ARMY – GENERAL JOHN J. PERSHING
I Corps – Major-General Hunter Liggett

1st Division – Major-General Charles Summerall; Colonel Campbell King, Chief of Staff
  - Divisional Command
    - 1st Machine-gun Battalion
    - 1st Engineer Battalion
    - 2nd Field Signal Battalion
  - 1st Brigade – Brigadier-General Frank Parker
    - 16th Infantry Regiment
    - 18th Infantry Regiment
    - 2nd Machine-gun Battalion
  - 2nd Brigade – Brigadier-General Frank Bamford
    - 26th Infantry Regiment
    - 28th Infantry Regiment
    - 3rd Machine-gun Battalion
  - 1st Field Artillery – Colonel Henry Butner
    - 5th Field Artillery (155mm)
    - 6th Field Artillery (75mm)
    - 7th Field Artillery (75mm)
    - 1st Trench Mortar Battery

42nd Division – Major-General Charles Menoher; Lieutenant-Colonel William Hughes, Chief of Staff
  - Divisional Command
    - 149th Machine-gun Battalion
    - 117th Engineer Battalion
    - 117th Field Signal Battalion
  - 83rd Brigade – Brigadier-General Michael Lenihan
    - 165th Infantry Regiment
    - 166th Infantry Regiment
    - 150th Machine-gun Battalion
  - 84th Brigade – Brigadier-General Douglas MacArthur
    - 167th Infantry Regiment
    - 168th Infantry Regiment
    - 151st Machine-gun Battalion
  - 67th Field Artillery – Brigadier-General George Gatley
    - 149th Field Artillery (75mm)
    - 150th Field Artillery(155mm)
    - 151st Field Artillery (75mm)
    - 117th Trench Mortar Battery

89th Division – Major-General William Wright; Lieutenant-Colonel Charles Kilbourne, Chief of Staff
  - Divisional Command
    - 340th Machine-gun Battalion
    - 314th Engineer Battalion
    - 314th Field Signal Battalion
  - 177th Brigade – Brigadier-General Frank Winn
    - 353rd Infantry Regiment
    - 354th Infantry Regiment
    - 341st Machine-gun Battalion
  - 178th Brigade – Brigadier-General Thomas Hanson
    - 355th Infantry Regiment
    - 356th Infantry Regiment
    - 342nd Machine-gun Battalion
  - 164th Field Artillery – Brigadier-General Edward Donnelly
    - 340th Field Artillery (75mm)
    - 341st Field Artillery (75mm)
    - 342nd Field Artillery (155mm)
    - 314th Trench Mortar Battery

IV Corps – Major-General Joseph Dickman

2nd Division – Major-General John Lejeune (USMC); Brigadier-General Preston Brown, Chief of Staff
  - Divisional Command
    - 4th Machine-gun Battalion
    - 2nd Engineer Battalion
    - 1st Field Signal Battalion
  - 3rd Brigade – Brigadier-General Hanson Ely
    - 9th Infantry Regiment
    - 23rd Infantry Regiment
  - 4th Brigade – Brigadier-General Wendell Neville (USMC)
    - 5th Marine Regiment
    - 6th Marine Regiment
  - 2nd Field Artillery – Brigadier-General Albert Bowley
    - 12th Field Artillery (75mm)
    - 15th Field Artillery (75mm)
    - 17th Field Artillery (155mm)
    - 2nd Trench Mortar Battery

5th Division – Major-General John McMahon; Colonel Clement Trott, Chief of Staff
  - Divisional Command
    - 13th Machine-gun Battalion
    - 7th Engineer Battalion
    - 9th Field Signal Battalion
  - 9th Brigade – Brigadier-General Joseph Castner
    - 60th Infantry Regiment
    - 61st Infantry Regiment
    - 14th Machine-gun Battalion
  - 10th Brigade – Colonel Paul Malone
    - 6th Infantry Regiment
    - 11th Infantry Regiment
    - 15th Machine-gun Battalion
  - 5th Field Artillery – Brigadier-General Clement Flagler
    - 19th Field Artillery (75mm)
    - 20th Field Artillery (75mm)
    - 21st Field Artillery (155mm)
    - 5th Trench Mortar Battery

82nd Division – Major-General William Burnham; Lieutenant-Colonel Boyden Beebe, Chief of Staff
  - Divisional Command
    - 319th Machine-gun Battalion
    - 307th Engineer Battalion
    - 307th Field Signal Battalion
  - 163rd Brigade – Brigadier-General Marcus Cronin
    - 325th Infantry Regiment
    - 326th Infantry Regiment
    - 321st Machine-gun Battalion
  - 164th Brigade – Brigadier-General Julian Lindsey
    - 327th Infantry Regiment
    - 328th Infantry Regiment
    - 322nd Machine-gun Battalion
  - 157th Field Artillery – Brigadier-General Charles Rhodes
    - 319th Field Artillery (155mm)
    - 320th Field Artillery (75mm)
    - 321st Field Artillery (75mm)
    - 307th Trench Mortar Battery

90th Division – Major-General Henry Allen; Colonel John Kingman, Chief of Staff
- Divisional Command
    - 343rd Machine-gun Battalion
    - 315th Engineer Battalion
    - 315th Field Signal Battalion
- 179th Brigade – Brigadier-General Paul O'Neil
    - 357th Infantry Regiment
    - 358th Infantry Regiment
    - 344th Machine-gun Battalion
- 180th Brigade – Brigadier-General Ulysses Alexander
    - 359th Infantry Regiment
    - 360th Infantry Regiment
    - 345th Machine-gun Battalion
- 165th Field Artillery – Brigadier-General Frances Marshall
    - 343rd Field Artillery (75mm)
    - 344th Field Artillery (75mm)
    - 345th Field Artillery (155mm)
    - 315 Trench Mortar Battery

V Corps – Major-General George Cameron

4th Division – Major-General John Hines; Lieutenant-Colonel Christian Bach, Chief of Staff
- Divisional Command
    - 10th Machine-gun Battalion
    - 4th Engineer Battalion
    - 8th Field Signal Battalion
- 7th Brigade: – Brigadier-General Benjamin Poore
    - 39th Infantry Regiment
    - 40th Infantry Regiment
    - 11th Machine-gun Battalion
- 8th Brigade – Brigadier-General Ewing Booth
    - 58th Infantry Regiment
    - 59th Infantry Regiment
    - 12th Machine-gun Battalion
- 4th Field Artillery – Major-General Edwin Babbitt
    - 13th Field Artillery (155mm)
    - 16th Field Artillery (75mm)
    - 77th Field Artillery (75mm)
    - 4th Trench Mortar Battery

26th Division – Major-General Clarence Edwards; Colonel Duncan Major, Chief of Staff
- Divisional Command
    - 101st Machine-gun Battalion
    - 101st Engineer Battalion
    - 101st Field Signal Battalion
- 51st Brigade – Brigadier-General George Shelton
    - 101st Infantry Regiment
    - 102nd Infantry Regiment
    - 102nd Machine-gun Battalion
- 52nd Brigade – Brigadier-General Charles Cole
    - 103rd Infantry Regiment
    - 104th Infantry Regiment
    - 103rd Machine-gun Battalion
- 51st Field Artillery – Colonel Otho Farr
    - 101st Field Artillery (75mm)
    - 102nd Field Artillery (75mm)
    - 103rd Field Artillery (155mm)
    - 101st Trench Mortar Battery

GERMAN

ARMY GROUP GALLWITZ – GENERAL MAX VON GALLWITZ
Army Detachment C – Lieutenant-General Georg Fuchs

Mihiel Group – Lieutenant-General Leuthold

5th Landwehr Division
- Divisional attachment
    - 16th Uhlan Regiment (two squadrons)
    - 405th Pioneer Battalion
    - 505th Signal Command
- 30th Landwehr Brigade
    - 25th Landwehr Regiment
    - 36th Landwehr Regiment
    - 65th Landwehr Regiment
- 256th Landwehr Field Artillery

192nd Saxon Division
- Divisional attachment
    - 18th Reserve Hussar Regiment (one squadron)
    - 192nd Pioneer Battalion
    - 192nd Signal Command
- 192nd Brigade
    - 183rd Regiment
    - 192nd Regiment
    - 245th Regiment
- 192nd Artillery Command
    - 192nd Field Artillery Regiment
    - 58th Saxon Field Artillery Battalion
    - 256th Landwehr Field Artillery Regiment

Gorze Group – General Hartz

10th Division
- Divisional attachment
    - 1st Horse Jäger Regiment (three squadrons)
    - 5th Pioneer Battalion
    - 10th Signal Command
- 20th Brigade
    - 6th Grenadiers
    - 47th Regiment
    - 398th Regiment
- 10th Artillery Command
    - 56th Field Artillery Regiment

77th Reserve Division
- Divisional Attachment
    - 2nd Horse Jäger Regiment (four squadrons)
    - 1st Pioneers (one company)
    - 77th Reserve Regiment
    - 332nd Regiment
    - 257th Reserve Regiment
    - 419th Regiment
- Artillery Command
    - 59th Reserve Artillery Regiment

Combres Group – General Below

8th Landwehr Division
- Divisional attachment
    - 5th Horse Jäger Regiment (one squadron)
    - 408th Pioneer Battalion
    - 508th Signal Command

56th Landwehr Brigade
     109th Landwehr Regiment
     110th Landwehr Regiment
     111th Landwehr Regiment
Artillery Command
     8th Landwehr Field Artillery Regiment

13th Landwehr Division
   Divisional attachment:
     6th Dragoon Regiment (five squadrons)
     413th Pioneer Battalion
   60th Landwehr Brigade
     15th Landwehr Regiment
     60th Landwehr Regiment
     82nd Landwehr Regiment
   Artillery Command
     13th Landwehr Field Artillery Regiment

35th Austro-Hungarian Division
   69th Infantry Brigade
     50th Regiment
     51st Regiment
   70th Infantry Brigade
     62nd Regiment
     63rd Regiment

Assigned to Army Detachment C from Metz Group
255th Division
   Divisional attachment
     7th Hussar Regiment (four squadrons)
     255th Pioneer Battalion
     255th Signal Command
   82nd Landwehr Brigade
     68th Landwehr Regiment
     94th Landwehr Regiment
     153rd Landwehr Regiment
   Artillery Command
     301st Field Artillery Regiment

Reserve units
123rd Saxon Division
   Divisional attachment
     20th Hussar Regiment (five squadrons)
     123rd Pioneer Battalion
     123rd Signal Command

245th Brigade
     178th Regiment
     106th Reserve Regiment
     351st Regiment
123rd Artillery Command
     137th Field Artillery Battalion

88th Division
   Divisional attachment
     10th Jäger zu Pferd (one squadron)
     88th Pioneer Battalion
     349th Pioneer Company
     Reserve Pioneer Battalion No. 33 (three companies)
   176th Brigade
     352nd Regiment
     353rd Regiment
     426th Regiment
   Artillery Command
     88th Field Artillery Regiment
     123rd Foot Artillery Battalion
31st Division
   Divisional attachment
     7th Uhlan Regiment (five squadrons)
     93rd Pioneer Battalion
   32nd Brigade
     70th Regiment
     166th Regiment
     174th Regiment
   31st Artillery Command
     31st Artillery Regiment
     44th Foot Artillery Battalion

195th Division
   Divisional attachment
     14th Uhlan Regiment (two squadrons)
     195th Pioneer Battalion
     195th Signal Command
   101st Reserve Brigade
     6th Jäger Regiment
     8th Jäger Regiment
     14th Jäger Regiment
   Artillery Command
     260th Field Artillery Regiment

OPPOSING PLANS

THE ST MIHIEL SALIENT

The French referred to the St Mihiel salient as "l'Hernie" ("the Hernia"). The western face was formed by the heights of the Meuse River. The town of St Mihiel formed the apex of the triangle and the southern face ran along flat ground toward the Moselle River. The salient was 25 miles wide at its base and approximately 15 miles deep.

The Germans constructed a strong defensive line, the Michel Stellung, composed of a reinforced first line and a less-developed second line, along the base of the salient, which ran between the towns of Haudiomont and Pont-à-Mousson. The defensive lines within the salient included the outer Wilhelm and inner Schroeter zones. To the northeast of the base was the Woëvre Plain. The salient was dominated by Montsec, rising over 2,500 feet above the surrounding countryside. Located 10 miles east of St Mihiel, Montsec provided the Germans with unlimited visibility across the American lines.

To the east of the St Mihiel salient was the Woëvre Plain, a large section of relatively open ground.

LEFT
Montsec dominated the surrounding countryside and provided the Germans with an unimpeded view of the American lines.

RIGHT
American troops under observation from Montsec. Although ruined villages did provide a minimum level of protection for small groups of men during daylight, major troop movements were undertaken at night to avoid detection.

Pershing and his staff had identified the possibilities for an attack against the St Mihiel salient in 1917 during preliminary discussions with the French high command over the initial deployment of the First US Army. The original American plan for reducing the salient, the August Plan, recognized that the salient threatened the security of the Paris–Nancy railroad and denied access to the railroad between St Mihiel and Verdun. Reducing the salient would provide a jumping-off point for a future attack on the Metz–Sedan railroad network, vital to the Germans' lateral communications and supply, and threaten the Briey Iron Basin, key to the production of German armaments and munitions. It would also allow the Americans to break out onto the Woëvre Plain. Preliminary planning emphasized surprise and speed, suggesting that if American forces maintained their momentum they would frustrate German efforts to launch a counterattack and might be able to breach the Michel Stellung before the Germans could effectively react. If that happened, an advance toward Metz seemed only logical.

The First US Army was formed on August 10, 1918, with its headquarters at La Ferte-sous-Jouarre. Pershing assumed direct command on August 25. Because of the previously agreed-upon shipment of only infantry and machine-gun units, the creation of the American force required supplemental provision of artillery and tanks from the French. The August agreement included 80 batteries of 75mm guns, 40 batteries of 155mm artillery, and 86 batteries of various other calibers. A week later Pershing increased his request to 100 75mm batteries and 50 155mm batteries. He also requested 150 heavy tanks and 300 light tanks, a portion of which were to be manned by two battalions of recently trained American personnel. Pershing also requested 21 squadrons of aircraft to support the offensive.

Timing for the offensive was driven by the anticipated arrival of wet fall weather in mid-September. In mid-August, Foch suggested that the attack on the salient begin on or about September 1, 1918, and involve 14 American divisions, supported by three or more French divisions. Pershing designated I, IV, and V corps for the St Mihiel attack. I Corps was still deployed on the Vesle River front, IV was at Toul, and V Corps was not fully organized. Pershing coordinated with General Pétain to expand Maj. Gen. Liggett's American I Corps to four divisions and to deploy Lieutenant-General Robert Bullard's III Corps adjacent to Liggett's troops.

Preliminary planning for the attack began on August 13, with the First Army staff considering three possible options. The Americans evaluated an attack on the southern face, an attack against the southern face in conjunction with a strike on the western face, and finally an attack on the nose of the salient. The attack against the nose was rejected as unfeasible, while a combined attack on the southern and western faces was given preliminary approval. As the plan evolved, 11 American divisions and 16 French divisions were to be committed in the attack. Foch gave the plans his approval on August 17 and offered to provide six additional French divisions.

The American plan of attack was to attack the flanks of the salient simultaneously, with the ultimate objective tentatively fixed as the Marieulles Heights south of Gorze–Mars-la-Tour–Etain. As originally developed, the plan proposed using three to four American divisions against the western face of the salient, supported by six divisions of the French Second Army on their left. Seven American divisions were assigned to attack the southern face of the salient and three French divisions would occupy the Germans' attention at the tip of the salient.

FOCH'S CHANGE OF PLANS

As Pershing and his staff worked feverishly to coordinate all the elements of the planned offensive, Foch and Haig were rethinking the strategy. In late August 1918 Haig had suggested to Foch that rather than looking toward 1919 as the decisive year, the German Army had been weakened enough that a general fall offensive might end the war. Haig proposed that the British Army attack in the direction of Cambrai, with the objective of breaching the Hindenburg Line and capturing the German railroad lines near Maubeuge. He also proposed that the First US Army support the British attack by advancing west of the Meuse River toward Mézières. Haig believed that the loss of the Maubeuge–Mézières railroad line, which supplied the Hindenburg Line, would cause Ludendorff to order a retreat to the German border. Foch was convinced of the advantages of a British attack on his left and an American offensive on the right and agreed with Haig.

As American planning for the St Mihiel offensive began to take shape, Foch met with Pershing on August 30, 1918. Pershing listened with growing dismay as Foch outlined his plan. Four to six American divisions were to be attached to the French Second Army to join in an attack between the Meuse River and Argonne Forest. An American army of eight to ten divisions would be assigned to attack northward in conjunction with the French Fourth Army along the Aisne. This realignment reduced the forces available for the St Mihiel attack to eight or nine divisions, and eliminated any expectation that the offensive could be a springboard for an advance against Metz or a breakout into the Woëvre Plain. Foch proposed that the reduced St Mihiel attack should begin no later than September 10. The advance in the Argonne would start on September 15 and the offensive along the Aisne would jump off on September 20.

More troubling to Pershing than the dilution of the American attack on St Mihiel was the suggestion that the First US Army would be split. Pershing challenged Foch's proposal, suggesting that the recently organized First US Army could undertake the St Mihiel attack and be available for further operations. Foch dismissed Pershing's concerns and suggested that the Germans were prepared to fall back if attacked, and that the commitment of the proposed American and French units would be unnecessary and divert resources from more-important objectives. Pershing argued that breaking up

American cavalry was used primarily as messengers and to patrol rear areas. During the afternoon of September 12, the provisional squadron of the 2nd Cavalry Regiment, attached to the 1st Division, was ordered to pursue retreating German forces toward Nonsard.

the newly organized First US Army would offend the American public, causing Foch to ask, "Do you wish to take part in the battle?" Pershing responded immediately, "Most assuredly, but as an American Army."

Foch responded to Pershing on September 1, reiterating his support for an attack west of the Meuse in the next several weeks. He also suggested that Pershing consider an attack against St Mihiel with a much-reduced force either prior to or simultaneous with the larger attack. Foch supported a limited attack along the southern face of the salient while Pershing believed that an assault should be directed against both the southern and western sides. Foch requested that Pershing attend a meeting the following day at Bombon to discuss the details of the attack west of the Meuse River.

While recognizing that Foch's proposal might result in either canceling the St Mihiel attack or postponing the larger offensive, Pershing suggested a third alternative. He proposed carrying out the St Mihiel offensive, limiting the advance to the Thiaucourt–Vigneulles line as Foch suggested but withdrawing as many divisions as possible for an attack in the Belfort or Lunéville regions. If Foch wanted American assistance in the attack on Mézières he pledged to commit an independent American force to an attack either east or west of the Argonne Forest.

At Bombon a compromise was reached, with Foch conceding the operation of an independent American army and Pershing agreeing to an attack between the Meuse and Argonne in coordination with the French Fourth Army. Foch agreed to push back the larger offensive until September 25 to allow the St Mihiel operation to be completed.

Pershing committed to attack the St Mihiel salient with eight to ten divisions on September 10 and halt at the Vigneulles–Thiaucourt–Regnéville line. He proposed shifting to the Meuse–Argonne attack, using 12 to 14 divisions in the initial attack and transferring additional resources from St Mihiel as they became available.

With the details resolved, Pershing's staff abandoned the August Plan, replacing it with the September Plan. Lieutenant-Colonel Hugh Drum, Chief of Staff of the First Army, and Lieutenant-Colonel James W. McAndrews, Chief of Staff of the General Headquarters, organized the logistics of moving and supplying the forces slated for the offensive. Lieutenant-Colonel George Marshall and Lieutenant-Colonel Walter S. Grant began work at the General Headquarters on the operations plan. In late August 1918 both men were transferred to First Army staff to assist Drum in the detailed planning.

The September Plan had much in common with the previous August Plan, calling for a principal attack on the southern face of the salient and a more limited effort against the western flank. The American IV Corps, commanded by Major-General Joseph Dickman, composed of the 89th, 42nd, and 1st divisions, was assigned to the principal attack in the south. The 3rd Division was assigned to Dickman as a reserve. The veteran 1st Division, deployed on the far left of the IV Corps sector, would be responsible for protecting the corps' flank, now left hanging in the air after French support was withdrawn. Although the French II Colonial Corps would launch deep raids against the Germans deployed at the nose of the salient, they would not undertake a general attack and would not be in position to protect IV Corps' left flank once they jumped off. IV Corps was directed to advance beyond Pannes on day one and then join V Corps at Vigneulles. The army plan included a first-

Map of the St Mihiel salient showing the locations of American and French units on September 11, 1918. The main American effort was intended to take place along the southern face of the salient.

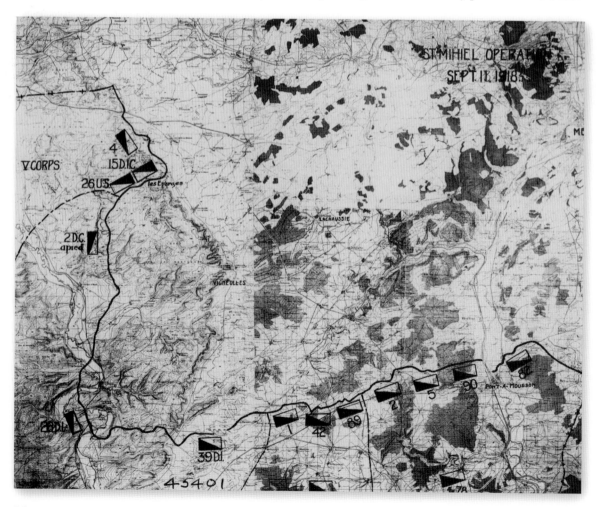

day objective for each division. It was expected that this position would be organized as the main line of resistance and, beginning on day two, American forces would push to the exploitation line, running parallel to the German Michel Stellung.

Speed was critical to the success of the plan. Marshall and his planners estimated that the Germans could begin reinforcing the salient with two divisions in two days and increase those numbers shortly afterwards. American intelligence anticipated a German counterattack from Metz, Etain, or Conflans during the first four days of the attack. If no serious German threat appeared during that period then Pershing would begin withdrawing units for the Meuse–Argonne offensive.

A central issue that both the operational planners and corps commanders struggled with was the amount of preparatory artillery fire. Some saw a thorough preparatory barrage as critical to destroying the bands of barbed wire the Germans had emplaced during their long occupation and for opening up lanes of attack, demoralizing the enemy defending the salient and restricting German attempts to organize a counterattack. Others pointed to the experience of the past year that suggested that the barrage would alert the enemy to the imminent attack and churn up the ground to such a degree that it would hinder the American advance and efforts to resupply units beyond the initial attack. The tank commanders, led by Lieutenant-Colonel Patton, were particularly concerned about the impact of the barrage on the ground over which they were expected to operate.

American planners debated the need for a prolonged initial artillery barrage. Lieutenant-Colonel Patton and others expressed concern that the impact of that barrage would be to reduce the ability of tanks to move across the disrupted terrain.

Three options were advanced, a full 14-hour preparatory barrage designed to remove any wire barriers, a shorter five-hour barrage directed primarily at enemy infantry concentrations, or forgoing the barrage entirely.

Marshall advocated the lengthy barrage, arguing that the British had reneged on providing their heavy tanks, which had been intended to cut corridors through the wire. Liggett argued that surprise and maneuverability were of primary importance and proposed no barrage.

Pershing initially agreed with Liggett but as the day of attack approached, pressed by Marshall and Grant, he reluctantly ordered a three-hour barrage along the southern flank and a seven-hour barrage along the west.

AMERICAN FORCES

Liggett's I Corps, made up of the 82nd, 90th, 5th, and 2nd divisions, supported by the 78th Division, was deployed to the east of IV Corps. It was deployed between the Bois-le-Prêtre and Limey and expected to reach the heights north of Thiaucourt by the end of the first day. The 82nd Division would remain in place and extend strong combat patrols against German strongpoints. The 90th Division, facing the Bois-le-Prêtre, was ordered to avoid a direct assault, skirting the wood on the west on day one and clearing it the following day. Both I Corps and IV Corps would attack at 0500hrs while V Corps would delay their advance until 0800hrs.

Major-General George Cameron's V Corps – including the 26th, a portion of the 4th, and the French 15th Colonial Division – would attack from the west toward Vigneulles and link up with Dickman's corps. The V Corps orders directed it to clear the Heights of the Meuse and advance to the Les Eparges–Mouilly–Ranzières line. The 26th Division would spearhead the advance, with the objective of driving southeast toward the first-day objective, a road between Longeau Farm and Dompierre. On day two the 26th was expected to reach Vigneulles.

The overall plan was fairly simple: IV Corps would drive north while the 26th Division of V Corps would advance southeast from their baseline with the goal of pinching off the salient by meeting forces advancing from the

Major-General Edwards (center), commander of the American 26th Division, and his staff. Edwards, a National Guard officer commanding a National Guard division, was frequently at odds with regular army leadership and staff.

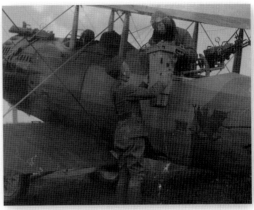

south at Vigneulles. Once the Germans in the nose of the salient were trapped, the French II Colonial Corps would move into St Mihiel and mop up. Meanwhile, the Americans would secure the line at Regnéville–Thiaucourt–Vigneulles and begin transitioning for the Meuse–Argonne offensive.

AIR FORCES

Colonel Billy Mitchell had been assigned the largest concentration of airpower in the history of warfare for the St Mihiel offensive. French, Italian, and Portuguese air elements were placed under the command of Mitchell and his First Air Service, while British air groups remained under a separate command. Mitchell's air assets included 1,500 coalition aircraft, including 701 pursuit airplanes, 366 observation airplanes, 323 day bombers, 91 night bombers, and 20 balloons.

On August 20, 1918, Mitchell established the organization and objectives for the coming air campaign. The aviation elements were organized into observation, pursuit, and bombardment groups. The attack was divided into four phases: preparation, night before the attack, day of the attack, and exploitation. The first objective was the destruction of the German air forces, followed by the reconnaissance of enemy positions, including the direction of artillery fire, and finally the destruction of enemy ground forces through bombardment and strafing.

Target selection was to be largely the responsibility of Mitchell and his staff, although flight commanders were given flexibility to use their discretion to attack targets of opportunity.

TANK FORCES

Brigadier-General Rockenbach was briefed by Colonel Drum at Neufchâteau on August 20, 1918, on the role anticipated for American armor in the St Mihiel attack. He was instructed to prepare plans for the participation of his two light-tank battalions, supplemented by a French light-tank regiment of three battalions and three British heavy-tank battalions, totaling over 500 tanks. Drum emphasized the need for the heavy tanks to break through the large concentrations of barbed wire that the American command believed protected the German positions. Patton, given command of the 1st Tank

Brigade, joined a French raid to conduct a reconnaissance of the St Mihiel battlefield on August 21, 1918.

On August 25 the British informed the Americans that they could not provide the heavy-tank battalions promised. As an alternative, the French committed the 1st Assault Artillery Brigade, composed of four battalions, totaling 300 Renault tanks. Rockenbach submitted a plan to First Army Command outlining the limited capabilities of his tank forces and reminding them not to base key objectives on their performance. Rockenbach assigned two French tank battalions to support I Corps on the right, the other two battalions in the center with IV Corps, and Patton's brigade on the left with V Corps. Patton established his brigade headquarters and issued detailed brigade orders on August 28. He also met with Major-Generals Clarence Edwards, commander of the 26th Division, and George Bell, commander of the 33rd Division, to discuss infantry coordination with the tanks. On September 3 Patton was forced to revise his plans when word reached him that his brigade was to be reassigned to support IV Corps on the southern face of the salient and the attack was postponed until September 12, 1918.

Plans for French tank support were also in flux. The French were sending the 505th Assault Artillery Regiment with three battalions, two St Chaumond-equipped company-sized units, and two Schneider-equipped companies. The Schneider-equipped units would be assigned to Patton. The tank force assigned to support the St Mihiel attack totaled 419. Patton revised his brigade plans, assigning the 327th Tank Battalion and the Schneider units to support the 1st Division, while the 326th Tank Battalion would support the attack of the 42nd Division.

The general reserve was composed of the 35th, 80th, and 91st divisions. Total American strength exceeded 550,000, while French strength totaled 110,000.

GERMAN DISPOSITIONS AND PLAN *LOKI*

The German high command had recognized the weakness of the St Michel salient since 1916. In that year they began construction of the Michel Stellung at the base of the salient, which was designed to serve as a fallback position. Ludendorff had engaged in discussions concerning the eventual evacuation of the salient. In June 1918 a German intelligence report predicted an attack on both faces of the salient and a holding action against the nose. The Germans assumed they would be able to recognize the signs leading to an American offensive and developed a withdrawal plan based on that premise. They assumed they would have about 12 days within which to react, using the first eight days to undertake the evacuation of important *matériel* and the destruction of defensive works.

The last part of the plan, codenamed *Loki*, assumed a withdrawal over four successive nights, accompanied by a scorched earth-strategy, including the systematic destruction of railroad lines. The plan included a phased withdrawal by the existing units, supported by security units and the designation of several reserve divisions intended to limit enemy penetrations and undertake limited counterattacks. To be safe, the Germans also prepared a backup plan, which assumed that they were in fact surprised by the offensive. Under that scenario the Germans would abandon the systematic destruction of facilities and *matériel* and focus instead on holding actions to secure the internal road network to allow for a withdrawal of the army over two nights.

The key to both phases of the withdrawal plans was the ability to collect good intelligence, which would allow the Germans to recognize in advance the anticipated attack and initiate the withdrawal. Despite mounting evidence that something was afoot, there was no hard information that confirmed the suspicions of the German staff. Throughout August aggressive German patrols probed the American lines, trying to gather information and capture prisoners. Although they were partially successful in identifying some of the American divisions deployed around the salient, they were frustrated in their attempts to take prisoners who could provide a broader source of detailed intelligence.

In early August 1918 the American activity around the salient was so widespread that German commanders thought it to be an all-too-obvious feint to draw their attention away from other fronts. The Germans suspected an American attack against the St Mihiel salient as early as September 1. Having failed to capture American prisoners with small-scale raids, the Germans launched a larger attack on an American outpost between Flirey and Limey early on the morning of September 7. The German raiding party, 200 men strong, followed a box barrage and attempted to encircle the outpost, which fell back on its supports. The defending American platoon drove off the raiding party, capturing several Germans who admitted that German commanders had requested volunteers for the raid without success.

On August 22, 1918, General Ludendorff assembled the Chief of Staff of the Army Group Gallwitz and Army Detachment C's Chief of Staff, Major-General Otto von Ledebur, at Imperial Headquarters at Avesnes. Ledebur detailed activity in French rear areas that pointed toward the assembly of supplies intended for a general offensive and suggested that the *Loki* movement be initiated.

German actions at the end of August and during the first two weeks of September reflected the contradictory thinking at higher levels of command. Beginning on August 25, Lt. Gen. Fuchs, anticipating an American attack, ordered heightened efforts to complete the defensive positions along the southern face of the salient. A September 1 German intelligence briefing noted the inactivity of American forces during August, and suggested that "it is not impossible that the American divisions are now held back in order to undertake an attack … under American command."

On September 3 General Max von Gallwitz informed the high command that he would order a withdrawal if the Americans launched a major attack. Despite the evidence that an attack was imminent, Gallwitz was still skeptical about its scope. He wrote that "indications and the enemy forces assumed to be opposite the south front of the army have not thus far pointed to enemy intentions to make a full-scale attack against the entire front of the army."

Gallwitz felt confident that he could resist a limited attack along the south flank of the salient with existing resources and prevail against a more determined assault if he was reinforced with several more divisions, was allocated additional artillery and machine guns, and had access to several counterattack divisions. After initially denying Gallwitz the additional resources, Ludendorff reversed his decision on September 7, giving permission to launch a spoiling attack on the southern flank "to shatter the enemy's offensive preparations." Fuchs planned an attack by six front-line divisions backed up by two reserve divisions, intended to push back the southern face of the salient to a line from Xivry to Pont-à-Mousson. While uncertain about the coming attack, directives were issued to units within the salient detailing their responsibilities. A September 8 order to the 10th Division spelled out the expectation that all units were to be on high alert, with carts available to immediately transfer documents, secret orders, and other important material to the rear. The order specified that the advanced zone was to be occupied by no more than one-third of unit strength. The task of the advance zone was to deny American patrols free movement and alert the main line of resistance to an American attack. The order reiterated that the main line of resistance should be held at all costs.

By September 9 Gallwitz was alerted to the continued American buildup and was noting mounting evidence that an attack would be launched from the western face of the salient. Ludendorff agreed, and on September 10 directed that action be taken to begin the phased withdrawal to the Michel Stellung. On his own initiative Fuchs began to prepare for the withdrawal and with subsequent agreement from Gallwitz and Ludendorff orders were issued to begin the preliminary stages of the movement. Gallwitz continued to hedge his bets, directing that demolition be limited and that if the situation changed the *Loki* movement phase would be canceled. He further directed that the main withdrawal could begin only on his order. Reflecting the growing sense of unease about American intentions, the Gorze Group was reinforced with the 31st Division on September 10 and the 88th Division was directed to take up positions near Gorze by the evening of September 13. The 123rd and 107th Saxon divisions were also put on alert and ordered to be ready to move into contact at short notice.

On September 11 Gallwitz submitted a lengthy assessment of the situation to Ludendorff. In it Gallwitz repeated the belief that the Americans were expected to attack the southern face of the salient at any time. He also anticipated the original American plan of attack by suggesting that the St Mihiel attack might be accompanied by a push from the Verdun area against the Briey Basin, threatening German lines of communication and a double envelopment of Metz.

DECEPTION

Although it was widely assumed that the Germans anticipated an American attack in the vicinity of St Mihiel as early as August 19, General Pétain wrote in some frustration to Pershing that the civilian population was already discussing the details of the anticipated attack. Pétain suggested to Pershing

that it might be worthwhile to attempt to confuse the Germans about the exact location of the attack. Pershing agreed and on August 22 directed Colonel Fox Conner, Col. Marshall, and Lt. Col. Walter Grant to initiate a very public reconnaissance in the upper-Alsace sector held by the French Seventh Army. Pershing then ordered Major-General Omar Bundy to assemble his corps staff at Belfort and begin planning an offensive in Alsace, 125 miles southeast of St Mihiel, against Mulhouse. Despite the frenzy of activity intended to deceive the Germans, Pershing admitted in an August 31 memorandum to Marshal Foch that "it now seems certain that the enemy is aware of the approaching attack."

With cooperation from the French, Bundy organized a credible effort to deceive the Germans. He brought together his staff and the reconnaissance officers from the seven divisions designated for the attack, increased aerial-reconnaissance flights, and expanded radio traffic. Only a few staff from the General Headquarters knew the exercise was a charade; even Bundy and his staff believed that they were planning an actual attack. More importantly, while the Germans were not entirely convinced, they were concerned enough to dispatch three additional divisions to reinforce the German defenses. Pershing played his part, traveling down to inspect the 29th Division, followed shortly by Pétain. The Germans responded to Pershing's visit by raiding the American lines the following morning, taking several prisoners. Keeping an eye on the Alsace region, Lt. Gen. Fuchs, commander of Army Detachment C, ordered expedited work on the Michel Stellung.

At the end of August, Conger arrived at Belfort and, in anticipation of the opening of the St Mihiel attack, ordered Bundy to pack up his headquarters. The delay in the opening of the attack forced Conger to return to Belfort, ordering Bundy to remain in place and expand his reconnaissance. While at Belfort, Conger, who assumed German spies were close by, intentionally left in his trash can a carbon copy of a letter to Pershing announcing that plans were set for an attack through the Belfort Gap. After going for a five-minute walk around his hotel he returned to find the trash can empty. French spies in Geneva reported that the Germans were responding to rumors of an attack by moving ammunition and artillery into fortresses along the Rhine. Everything was now in place and the stage set for the St Mihiel attack.

ST MIHIEL

With the approval of the revised plans for the attack, the movement of over 500,000 troops began. To maintain some semblance of secrecy, movement toward the front of combat units and concentrations of supplies took place primarily at night. In order not to attract German attention a certain level of daytime activity was maintained and increased slightly during the first week of September. While the Germans did anticipate a possible attack against the salient, their intelligence reports estimated that given the character and amount of observed traffic circulation the offensive most likely had been postponed.

The rains came early in September, drenching the men as they marched in pitch-black night toward the front and slept in the woods during the day. The rain continued over the night of September 11–12, filling the trenches at the front with water and mud and further hampering the movement of troops and supplies.

As early as September 8 American intelligence began to detect signs that a German withdrawal might be under way. A prisoner captured on September 8 reported that the narrow-gauge railroads were being removed. On September 11 aerial reconnaissance reported no hostile fire from forward German trenches, raising further suspicions. Alternatively, the radio-intelligence section reported normal German radio traffic throughout the day.

By September 10 the 89th and 90th divisions had narrowed their frontages to allow the additional units to move to the front. The combination of rain together with thousands of men and hundreds of trucks moving toward the front turned every road and path into a quagmire. Once at the front the troops were assigned to waterlogged trenches and prohibited from lighting fires or smoking. Pershing held a final meeting of all corps commanders at Ligny on September 10. Several staff recommended a delay because of the soggy ground conditions, but given the tight timetable required to get the First US Army positioned for the Meuse–Argonne offensive, Pershing rejected the suggestion.

DEPLOYMENT

I Corps
The American I Corps, commanded by Maj. Gen. Liggett, held the easternmost portion of the line, with its right resting at Pont-à-Mousson. From east to west I Corps had the 82nd Division deployed on both banks of the Moselle, with the 90th, 5th, and 2nd divisions extending to Limey. The 78th Division was assigned as corps reserve. I Corps was directed to capture Thiaucourt and assist IV Corps in capturing the Bois d'Euvezin and Bois du Beau-Vallon.

German and American deployment, St Mihiel salient, September 12, 1918

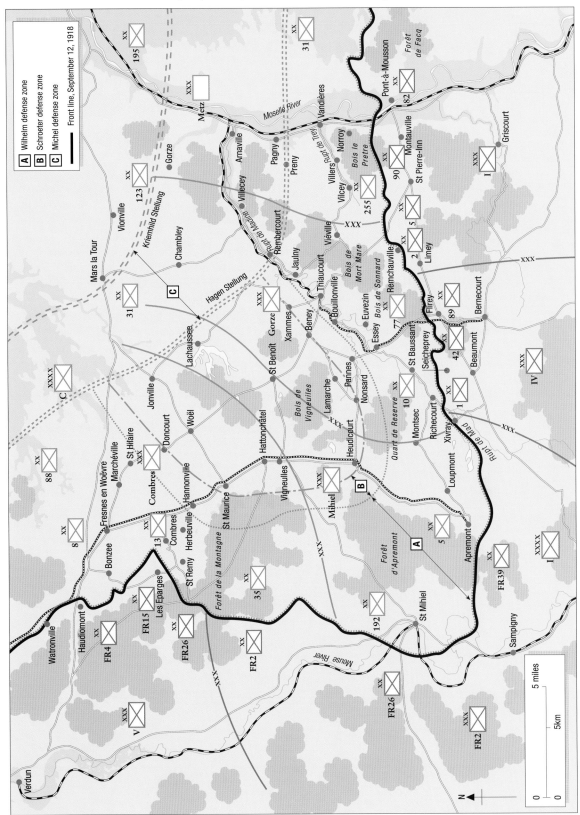

The **2nd Division** was deployed on the extreme left of the corps' line, with the 5th Division to its right and the 89th Division from IV Corps on the left. The 3rd Brigade, composed of the 9th and 23rd regiments, was designated to lead the assault, followed by the 4th Brigade, made up of the 5th and 6th Marine regiments. The first-day objectives for the division included an initial advance of 3 miles to the first objective line at the Bois de Heiche, where it would reorganize and move almost 2 miles farther to the second objective line along a line crossing the Rupt de Mad, between Thiaucourt and Jaulny, before stopping for the night.

The **82nd Division**, positioned on the easternmost flank of the American line, straddling the Moselle River, was expected to "exert pressure on and maintain contact with the enemy" and was not expected to undertake any significant offensive actions. Liggett, commanding I Corps, argued without success that the 82nd should move forward and threaten a concentration of German guns at Vittonville.

The **90th Division** occupied a frontage of roughly 3 miles and formed the easternmost attack element of I Corps. The I Corps attack plans designated the 90th Division to advance in line with the 5th and 2nd divisions, while protecting the corps' right flank. The divisional attack orders prescribed that the two brigades would deploy side by side, and that within each brigade the regiments would also be deployed in line. The entire division was expected to pivot on the right flank, with the 180th Brigade on the right merely holding its ground while the 179th Brigade advanced, keeping contact with the 5th Division on its left. The 179th Brigade was ordered to advance roughly 2 miles to reach the first-day objective.

The **5th Division**, positioned between the 2nd Division and 90th Division, held a narrow front just over a mile wide. The division was directed to drive due north, capturing the ruined village of Viéville, which lay just beyond the American lines. The first German position, which included bands of barbed wire and a system of trenches, was located a half-mile beyond Regnéville near the Bois de la Rappe. The second position, almost a mile farther north, was considered the main line of resistance. Stretching through the Bois des Saulx, Grandes Portions, and St Claude, this position was composed of two trenchlines reinforced with concrete strongpoints. The Germans had also constructed deep dugouts in the woods and had deployed artillery north of

General John Lejeune and 2nd Division staff.

the woods. Viéville had been reinforced with machine-gun positions in abandoned houses and in the steeple of a church. A German hospital and rest camp was located in the third German line, almost 2 miles beyond Viéville.

IV Corps

Commanded by Maj. Gen. Dickman, IV was made up of the 89th, 42nd, and 1st divisions, tied in with the French II Colonial Corps, which was positioned opposite the nose of the salient. The 3rd Division was held as corps reserve. The corps was expected to drive on St Benoît and Vigneulles and assist I Corps in capturing Thiaucourt. If I Corps was delayed then IV Corps was authorized to capture Thiaucourt.

The Bois de Mort Mare and adjacent Bois de la Sonnard extended almost across the entire frontage of the **89th Division**. To the east of the forest the Promenade des Moines, a bare ridge, dominated the landscape. The slope to the top of the ridge was covered with trenches and barbed wire. There were two strongpoints: Robert Mesnil Farm and Ansoncourt Farm. Extending northeast of the Bois de Mort Mare were the dense woods of the Bois d'Euvezin and Bois du Beau-Vallon. A narrow-gauge railroad traversed the Bois de Mort Mare.

Attack orders directed a general advance toward Euvezin with the intention of supporting the movement of the 42nd Division on the west and the 1st Division on the east. The 89th Division was ordered to capture Thiaucourt if the 1st Division was delayed.

Major-General Wright assumed command of the division on September 6. Wright affirmed the preliminary staff planning, which focused the main effort of the division to assist 42nd Division on the west. The 178th Brigade was deployed on the left. The 177th Brigade, less the 354th Regiment, which was designated as divisional reserve, was to support the 1st Division on the east. The 178th Brigade planned on advancing through the Bois de la Sonnard and Bois de Mort Mare, using two open corridors, each 200yds wide. The 177th Brigade would bypass the Bois de Mort Mare to the east on the first day and detach units as necessary in order to clear out any lingering resistance in the woods.

The **1st Division** occupied the extreme left flank of the American line on the southern face of the salient. The 2nd Brigade (26th and 28th regiments) was deployed on the right, maintaining contact with the 42nd Division while

TOP
American tanks and crews deployed for the St Mihiel attack. Patton developed a system for identifying companies using symbols such as diamonds or hearts painted on the tanks.

BOTTOM
Brigadier-General MacArthur and staff. MacArthur commanded a brigade in the 42nd Division.

the 1st Brigade (16th and 18th regiments) was placed on the left. The third battalions of each infantry regiment were assigned as either brigade or division reserve. Both brigades occupied a front approximately 2 miles wide and were expected to advance a little over 4 miles, capturing the Quart de Reserve and the town of Nonsard. All front-line infantry was to be accompanied by engineer detachments, equipped with Bangalore torpedoes and special bridging equipment for crossing the Rupt de Mad and Rupt de Madine. Additional specially equipped infantry units were equipped with wire-cutters. The divisional plan included four phases, each governed by a rolling artillery barrage. Each phase had a separate objective that allowed the infantry to reorganize. The barrage was scheduled to pause briefly before continuing. Premature advances beyond each objective would subject the infantry to friendly fire and once the fourth objective was reached the division was expected to consolidate its position for the night. The 1st Division advance was to be supported by 120 75mm guns and 48 155mm or 8in. howitzers. An elaborate schedule for displacing individual batteries forward to maintain the barrage was also prepared. The division was assigned 49 tanks, which were deployed along the left flank, and a detachment of cavalry.

The **42nd Division** moved to the front during the night of September 10–11, deploying between the 1st Division and 89th Division. The division objective was from the Bois de Dampvitoux, north of St Benoît, through the Bois de Vignette. The division deployed its regiments in line across its frontage. While the division was considered one of the most combat tested in the First US Army, the losses of the Aisne–Marne fighting earlier in the summer had depleted its ranks. Some battalions would begin the attack with replacement men and officers making up more than 50 percent of their strength.

TOP
The 26th Division was ordered to advance through the wire toward the devastated Bois Eparges. Neither the German wire nor the Bois Eparges represented a significant barrier to the initial advance of the 26th Division.

BOTTOM
General John Pershing, center, reviewing Maj. Gen. Cameron's 26th Division.

American tanks loaded onto railroad cars for transport to the front.

V Corps

Deployed on the western face at Les Eparges, V Corps positioned the 26th Division, the French 15th Colonial Division, and the 8th Brigade of the 4th Division. The remainder of the 4th Division was assigned as corps reserve. The corps was assigned the task of capturing the Heights of the Meuse, focusing on Les Eparges, Combres, and Amaranthe.

The **26th Division** joined Maj. Gen. Cameron's V Corps on August 28, 1918, settling into position along a 2½-mile front between the French 15th Colonial Division to the north and the 2nd Dismounted Cavalry Division to the south. The 26th Division's objective was to secure the Heights of the Meuse and pivot to its left, bringing its right flank into line with the American units advancing from the south, and ultimately move toward the Michel Stellung.

Tank support

Patton's final attack plans directed that his 1st Tank Brigade, with 144 Renault tanks and joined by two groups of French Schneider tanks, would be used to support the 1st Division and 42nd Division. The 327th Tank Battalion, led by Captain Ranulf Compton, would be supported by the French 14th and 17th groups and would support the 42nd Division. Major Sereno Brett's 326th Tank Battalion would be assigned to the 1st Division. Patton also instituted an identification protocol based on the suites of playing cards. Hearts, diamonds, clubs, and spades were stenciled on white backgrounds on each tank's turret. A number between one and five was also marked next to the symbol to identify each tank in a platoon.

THE ATTACK BEGINS

As the Americans struggled through the rain to reach their jump-off positions or waited with anticipation for the attack to begin, Lt. Gen. Fuchs had already issued orders to the 10th Division and 77th Reserve Division to begin their withdrawal. He directed both divisions to fall back to the artillery protective line by 0300hrs, leaving limited forces behind to delay any American advance.

At 0100hrs, September 12, 1918, in a driving, cold rain, the first American offensive began with the firing of thousands of artillery pieces all along the St Mihiel salient. German artillery returned fire, concentrating on the American front line and strategic targets such as crossroads to the rear of the front lines. Although the German artillery fire was sporadic and largely ineffective, it did catch the ammunition supply train of the 2nd Division and inflicted severe casualties. Reports from along the line remarked that German fire was largely negligible and American counterbattery fire silenced the few German guns that attempted to reply. Colonel "Wild Bill" Donovan, a veteran of fighting along the Ourcq and Vesle rivers, understood the implication, remarking simply, "The Germans are pulling out."

As the American artillery increased in tempo, so did the flow of men and vehicles toward the front. Tanks intended to support the 5th Division, along with an artillery ammunition train, became entangled in a massive traffic jam. Some units were safely in position by midnight but others struggled through the rain, mud, and chaos toward the front. Men from the 9th Regiment, 2nd Division, waded through thigh-deep water for almost a mile before reaching their positions. Patton's tanks were detrained and moved slowly toward the front. In the 1st Division sector five tanks accompanied the infantry toward the Rupt de Mad while 44 others deployed on the left, crossing the stream behind American lines and moving to support the attack. American air squadrons waited impatiently throughout the night, watching the rain and listening to the artillery, unsure whether they would be released to fly in the horrible weather.

German reaction

Major-General Otto von Ledebur, Army Detachment C's Chief of Staff, rushed to his headquarters at Conflans to piece together the details of the American attack. The American barrage had caught the 10th and 77th Reserve divisions in the process of pulling back to the artillery protective line. The German 10th Division had mixed success in withdrawing. Having deployed its artillery in deep echelon, it was able to avoid serious losses, and the bulk of the infantry also escaped the initial barrage. Conversely, the commander of the 77th Reserve Division delayed the withdrawal of his

An American ammunition truck being camouflaged. The use of camouflage had become widespread by both the Allies and Germans by 1918. Intricate patterns were used on vehicles, airplanes, and artillery. The Germans also pioneered the use of camouflage on helmets.

American advance, September 12–16, 1918

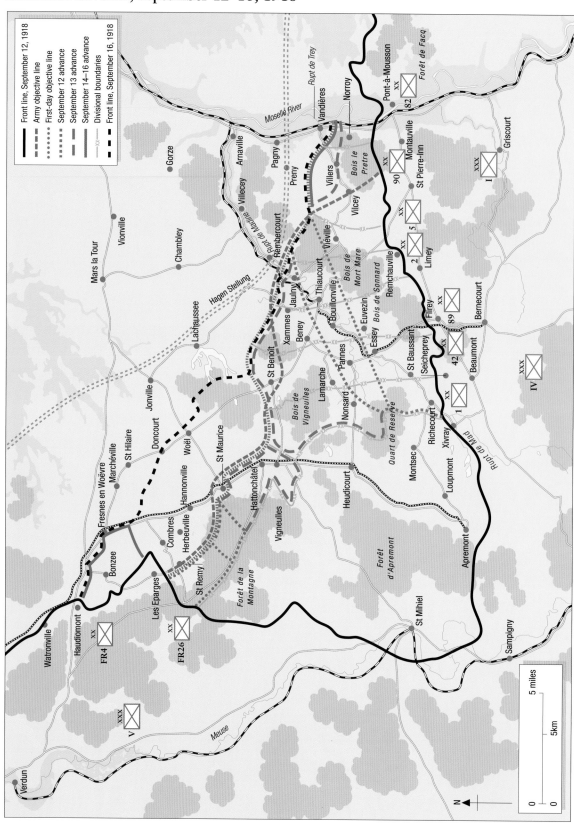

Front line, September 12, 1918
Army objective line
First-day objective line
September 12 advance
September 13 advance
September 14–16 advance
Divisional boundaries
Front line, September 16, 1918

Operations of the 42nd and 89th divisions, September 12, 1918

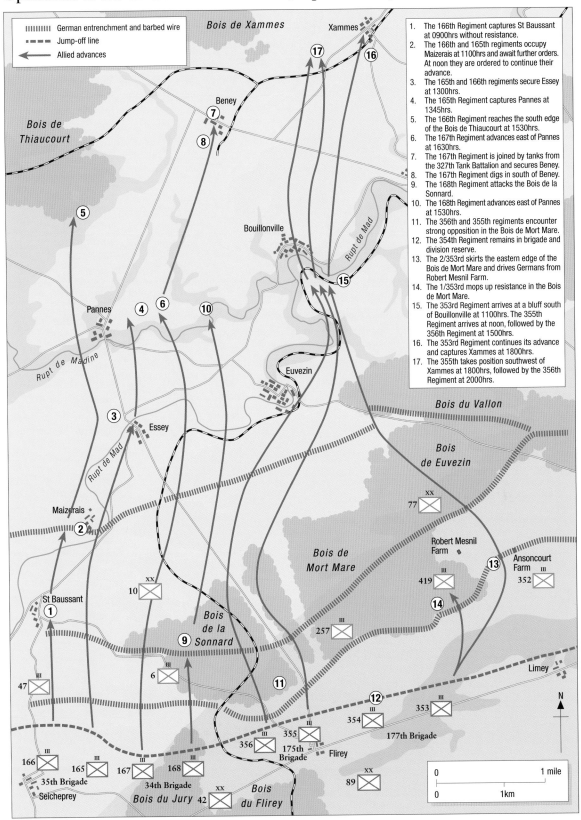

Legend:
- IIIIIIIII German entrenchment and barbed wire
- ▪▪▪▪ Jump-off line
- ← Allied advances

1. The 166th Regiment captures St Baussant at 0900hrs without resistance.
2. The 166th and 165th regiments occupy Maizerais at 1100hrs and await further orders. At noon they are ordered to continue their advance.
3. The 165th and 166th regiments secure Essey at 1300hrs.
4. The 165th Regiment captures Pannes at 1345hrs.
5. The 166th Regiment reaches the south edge of the Bois de Thiaucourt at 1530hrs.
6. The 167th Regiment advances east of Pannes at 1630hrs.
7. The 167th Regiment is joined by tanks from the 327th Tank Battalion and secures Beney.
8. The 167th Regiment digs in south of Beney.
9. The 168th Regiment attacks the Bois de la Sonnard.
10. The 168th Regiment advances east of Pannes at 1530hrs.
11. The 356th and 355th regiments encounter strong opposition in the Bois de Mort Mare.
12. The 354th Regiment remains in brigade and division reserve.
13. The 2/353rd skirts the eastern edge of the Bois de Mort Mare and drives Germans from Robert Mesnil Farm.
14. The 1/353rd mops up resistance in the Bois de Mort Mare.
15. The 353rd Regiment arrives at a bluff south of Bouillonville at 1100hrs. The 355th Regiment arrives at noon, followed by the 356th Regiment at 1500hrs.
16. The 353rd Regiment continues its advance and captures Xammes at 1800hrs.
17. The 355th takes position southwest of Xammes at 1800hrs, followed by 356th Regiment at 2000hrs.

artillery, resulting in the destruction of the bulk of the guns. Ignoring orders to reduce the number of men deployed in forward positions, the 77th Reserve Division was caught with nearly two-thirds of its men in the front lines.

Lieutenant-General Fuchs correctly concluded that the strong American artillery barrage heralded an attack against the southern face of the salient. At 0130hrs, without authority from Supreme Headquarters, he directed the 123rd and 31st divisions, deployed in reserve, to concentrate north of Charey and around Gorze. Fearing the worst, he also notified the 88th Division to move to Allamont and the 107th Division to move to Buzy. Fuchs was later given command of the 255th Division deployed along the Moselle.

OVER THE TOP

IV Corps

At 0500hrs the artillery shifted back toward the German front-line positions, and along the southern face of the salient whistles sounded as the Americans rose up and advanced. With their appearance, multicolored flares rose over the German positions.

On the far left of the southern face of the salient, under the unflinching gaze of Montsec, the 1st Division moved out, each front-line platoon accompanied by sections of engineers equipped with wire-cutters or Bangalore tubes to open paths through the German wire. In addition, other engineer details carried bridging equipment to cross the Rupt de Mad. On the division's extreme left the 18th Regiment deployed two battalions in line and was supported by tanks and a provisional squadron of the 2nd Cavalry. The 16th, 28th, and 26th regiments extended the 1st Division line to the east. Following the barrage the 1st Division paused briefly at its first objective, the southern bank of the Rupt de Mad, before splashing across the creek and moving toward the ruins of Richecourt and past its second objective. Pushing past feeble German resistance in Richecourt, they continued through Lahayville toward the third objective line; as they neared the southern edge of the Quart de Reserve the woods became alive with German machine-gun fire. Supported by tanks, the infantry rushed through the improvised barbed wire, capturing or killing the defenders.

The 1st Division advancing under the shadow of Montsec. Montsec dominated the St Mihiel battlefield, allowing German observers to monitor the movements of American troops along the southern face of the salient.

American infantry and tanks advance near Seicheprey. American troops had been assigned around the Seicheprey area since the spring of 1918. In April 1918 the Germans launched a major raid on 1/102nd Regiment of the American 26th Division, capturing 187 men and killing 81. The raid was a major embarrassment for the Americans, and set back General Pershing's attempts to organize an independent American army.

Earlier in the morning Patton had reported to IV Corps headquarters from his observation point, a hill northwest of Seicheprey, that only five of his tanks were out of action. In reality Compton's 325th Battalion had only 25 tanks actively engaged; 23 were out of action because of mechanical failures or from being stuck in mud. Another 19 were assigned either to resupply duties or as part of the battalion reserve.

Skirting the woods where German resistance was too strong, the 1st Division reached its third objective between 0930 and 1000hrs. Light-artillery batteries were pushed forward to cover the next phase of advance by 1100hrs. As the 1st Division approached the third objective line, IV Corps issued orders to secure the first-day objective, enemy positions between La Marce and Nonsard, as soon as possible. At 1100hrs, with renewed artillery support, the support battalions passed through the assault battalions and led the advance through the enemy wire, which proved far less of a barrier than feared. The infantry forded the Rupt de Madine, but the supporting tanks found the steep bank problematic and several became disabled. By 1230hrs, led by a platoon of tanks from Major Brett's 326th Tank Battalion, the 1st Division had captured Nonsard, securing the first-day objective. Brett's tanks rooted out the sporadic German defenders, destroying a machine gun hidden in a church steeple with their 37mm guns. The reserve battalions and machine-gun companies were moved forward to defend against the expected German counterattack. The provisional squadron of the 2nd Cavalry was also moved forward to exploit any breakthrough.

Captain Eddie Rickenbacker described the scene from the air as he flew over the southern face of the salient during the morning of September 12:

Closely pressing came our eager doughboys fighting along like Indians. They scurried from cover to cover, always crouching low as they ran. Throwing themselves flat onto the ground, they would get their rifles into action and spray the Boches with more bullets until they withdrew from sight. Then another running advance and another furious pumping of lead from the Yanks.

To the east of the 1st Division the 42nd Division also advanced, with all four regiments in line with one battalion designated as assault, one as support, and one as reserve. The 83rd Brigade, composed of the 166th Ohio and 165th New York regiments, formed on the left while the 84th Brigade with the 167th Alabama and 168th Iowa regiments deployed on the right. Engineering squads were assigned to each assault battalion to open gaps in the wire and facilitate the crossing of streams and trenches by tanks and artillery. Initial orders directed the division to secure the second objective line, running from northeast of Nonsard, south of Lamarche, and north of Thiaucourt, by the end of the first day.

The 42nd Division pushed off at 0500hrs and found the German wire rusted and easily overcome. The division's 83rd Brigade and the 167th Alabama advanced without serious resistance. The 3/168th Iowa ran into the German 6th Grenadier Regiment of the 10th Division in the Bois de Sonnard. The Iowans were slowed by bands of new barbed wire and strong resistance from German machine guns. The assault battalion took cover and began to suffer from sporadic *Minenwerfers*, which blew huge craters among the infantry. The American tanks lumbered through the mud and shellholes toward the wood as the Iowa officers cajoled their men to advance quickly and use their bayonets. Captain Dean Gilfillan, commander of Company A, 327th Tank Battalion, led a platoon of tanks toward the wood and knocked out several machine-gun positions. Company M on the far left of the Iowa line lost all its officers while Company K was left with just one lieutenant. On the right, led by the twice-wounded battalion commander, Major Guy Brewer, the 3/168th broke into the woods and rushed at the Germans in the trenches with bayonets. It was over in a matter of minutes and by 0630hrs word was received that the woods were secure. The action cost the 3/168th over 200 casualties while taking over 300 German prisoners from the 6th Grenadier and 47th regiments.

The rest of the 42nd Division continued forward, meeting little resistance. The 3/166th Ohio pushed aside weak resistance at St Baussant, capturing the

American tanks suffered from mechanical breakdowns and the difficulties of moving through water-soaked terrain. This tank is being removed from a ditch.

village with few casualties. Company M was assigned the task of rounding up the Germans hiding throughout the village while the rest of the battalion moved across the Rupt de Mad and toward Maizerais. At the same time the 1/165th New York moved toward the village on the right. The 1/165th advance was stalled by German defense of the stone bridge over the Rupt de Mad. Ordering mortar and 37mm fire to tie down the defenders, Colonel Donovan forded the stream with a platoon and captured 40 men, one mortar, and four machine guns.

By 1100hrs the first objective line had been reached. At noon, orders came to continue the advance and the 42nd moved quickly toward Essey. Elements of both the 1/165th and 3/166th, supported by a section of French Schneider tanks and tanks from the 327th Tank Battalion, advanced against Essey. Patton, who had spent the morning trying to keep in touch with Compton's 327th Tank Battalion, joined the infantry south of the village. Patton conferred with Brigadier-General Douglas MacArthur on a small hill, watching the German retreat.

By this time several groups of American tanks were approaching the town and Patton directed a platoon into Essey, followed by MacArthur and Donovan's 1/165th infantry. After securing the village, Donovan sheltered his men in walled gardens to protect them from random artillery rounds. French civilians and groups of Germans bailed out of their dugouts and surrendered to the infantry and supporting tanks. The supporting battalion, 2/165th, began organizing the prisoners and collecting captured material, including several barrels of beer, which Colonel Anderson, commander of the 2/165th, ordered destroyed.

MacArthur and Patton continued their advance toward Pannes, passing the remains of German artillery, men, and horses that had been caught in the American artillery barrage. Patton and several of his tanks pushed through Pannes, heading for Beney. German machine-gun fire riddled the turret of the tank Patton was riding, forcing him to take cover in a nearby shellhole. After unsuccessfully requesting support from the nearby infantry, Patton caught up with the single tank and guided it back to Pannes.

By 1230hrs the remainder of the tank platoon arrived and a coordinated assault was organized. The 3/166th supported Patton's tanks in a direct approach to Beney while the 3/167th outflanked the village on the right. A platoon of 3/167th accompanied by tanks entered Beney, cleared the town, and continued to the Bois de Beney. The infantry and tanks captured 16 machine guns and a battery of four 77mm guns in Beney. Donovan's infantry, accompanied by the tanks, moved through Pannes, headed for the second

LEFT
The FT-17 Renault tank spearheaded the American advance of the 1st and 42nd divisions.

RIGHT
Captain Eddie Rickenbacker was a popular automotive racecar driver before joining the Army and eventually entering the Army Air Service. Already an ace, Rickenbacker would shoot down an enemy aircraft on both September 14 and 15.

objective line, the Bois de Thiaucourt, to the west of Beney. Supported by Patton's tanks, the 1/165th drove the Germans from the woods and secured the Bois de Thiaucourt.

In Pannes the American infantry discovered a German quartermaster's storehouse, yielding a treasure trove of souvenirs including pistols, spurs, hats, helmets, underwear, and musical instruments. The Germans waited for their captors in their dugouts. One German was found with a bottle of schnapps and a glass; he immediately offered his captor a drink, saying, "I don't drink it myself, but I thought it would be a good thing to offer to an American who would find me."

The 89th Division, on the far right of IV Corps, was expected to attack in the direction of Euvezin, keeping pace with the 42nd Division on its left and 2nd Division on the right. The 89th Division's placement opposite the Bois de Mort Mare reflected the overall strategy of the First Army: to direct the veteran divisions across open ground where they could move quickly to exploit German weakness while the less experienced divisions would engage the Germans deployed in the woods. The Bois de Mort Mare, an extension of the Bois de Sonnard that caused the 42nd Division difficulties, masked the entire front of the 89th Division with the exception of two narrow open strips north of Flirey. Division staff decided to have the 177th Brigade flank the wood on the east. The 354th Regiment was detached from the 177th Brigade to form the brigade and divisional reserve.

The 178th Brigade, occupying twice the frontage of the 177th, was deployed on the left and tasked with forcing its way through the wood. At 0500hrs the 3/355th and 3/356th regiments, deployed side by side, moved directly toward the Bois de Mort Mare through a storm of artillery and machine-gun fire. Officers leading from the front were struck down as both regiments approached the southern edge of the wood. Rushing forward, the Americans overran the first German trench, a second trench deep in the wood, and finally a trench along the wood's northern edge. American casualties were severe, particularly among officers. The 356th Regiment captured over 100 Germans, mostly from the 257th Regiment of the 77th Reserve Division.

Men of the 42nd Division and American tanks moving through Essey. It was near Essey that Brig. Gen. MacArthur and Col. Patton met briefly and chatted while enduring a German artillery barrage.

On the right, the 2/353rd Regiment, 177th Brigade, skirted the Bois de Mort Mare, taking fire from Germans in the wood and from the Ansoncourt Farm at the southern edge of the Bois d'Euvezin. By 0515hrs every officer in Company E was killed or wounded, but despite taking over 200 casualties word was sent back that Ansoncourt Farm had been captured and that the Americans were entering the wood. Infantry from both the 355th and 353rd regiments slowly made their way through the dense underbrush, avoiding the trails and paths, which they suspected were registered by the German machine guns. Outflanking the enemy guns, the Americans methodically cleared the wood, showing little mercy to those gunners who fired until surrounded, but capturing hundreds of the enemy before stopping at the northern edge of the forest. The 2/353rd continued into the Bois du Beau-Vallon, taking another 200 prisoners and 15 machine guns. At the northern edge of Vallon the 3/353rd advanced through the battle-weary 2nd Battalion and took up the advance.

Following behind the assault battalion, the 1/353rd cleared German resistance in the Bois de Mort Mare, capturing Germans who were surprised that they had been surrounded. Private Joseph Szczepanik, advancing alone, gathered 150 German prisoners from their dugouts before being wounded. Both woods were secured by 0800hrs.

Advancing north from the wood, both brigades re-established contact and moved to the heights north of Euvezin, where they halted to reorganize. At 1100hrs the 3/353rd reached the first objective line, south of Bouillonville, and waited while the 1/355, moving up to replace the 3/355th as assault

Men of Iron by Don Troianni. Although German resistance was sporadic, fierce battles took place in the Bois de Mort Mare between American infantry and German defenders.

COMBINED-ARMS ATTACK ON BENEY, SEPTEMBER 12, 1918 (pp. 50–51)

Lieutenant-Colonel Patton accompanied elements of the 326th and 327th tank battalions in their advance on September 12. In the late morning Patton directed tank operations against Essey and Pannes in conjunction with infantry elements of the 42nd Division. After securing Pannes, Patton rode on the rear deck of an American tank as it moved toward Beney. German machine-gun fire drove him off to find cover with infantry of the 167th Regiment. Failing to convince the infantry commander to accompany his lone tank in an attack on Beney, Patton was forced to order the tank to return to his position. At 1230hrs four additional tanks arrived and Patton convinced the infantry commander to accompany them in a coordinated attack. The attack stalled short of the town when the infantry moved into the Bois de Thiaucourt. Patton ordered the tanks to follow. At 1400hrs two additonal tanks joined Patton's force and with another platoon from the 167th Regiment the American tanks and infantry captured Beney in the late afternoon.

Patton **(1)** is shown standing next to the FT-17 Renault tank **(2)**, gesturing toward Beney. Men from an infantry platoon from the 167th Infantry Regiment mill around the tank platoon, wearing raincoats to protect them from the rain **(3)**. The soldier in the foreground is armed with a Winchester shotgun **(4)**. The Winchester Model 97, with pump action, fired a 12-gauge shell from a six-round magazine. The effectiveness of the shotgun in clearing German trenches and defensive positions resulted in the German government lodging a formal protest with the American government in September 1918, claiming that the weapon violated the terms of the Hague Convention, a forerunner to the Geneva Convention. The protest was rejected.

The repair of roads was critical to assuring that supplies and supporting artillery could move forward to support the American advance.

battalion, moved up on their left. The 3/356th failed to keep pace, delayed by thick woods and prolonged German resistance, and would not reach the front until 1500hrs.

The 89th Division commander, Maj. Gen. Wright, who had moved his headquarters to Flirey at 1000hrs, set about moving the divisional artillery beyond the Bois de Mort Mare. Engineers were ordered to improve the road north from Flirey and a regiment of artillery was deployed north of the Bois de Mort Mare by mid-afternoon. At the same time, Wright received revised orders from I Corps directing his division to continue its advance to the army objective. The revised objective line extended from the center of the Bois de Dampvitoux, 2½ miles north of Beney, to Xammes. To occupy this line the 89th Division would have to wheel left to the northeast, using Xammes as the pivot.

While waiting for the 178th Brigade to come up, the 3/353rd sent out patrols, which immediately drew scattered machine-gun and artillery fire. Brushing aside the German defenders, the 3/356th entered the town, finding hundreds of German 10th Division support personnel waiting patiently to surrender to someone. Sergeant Harry Adams followed a German soldier to a dugout built into a hillside. After firing his last two bullets from his pistol into the door he demanded that they surrender. Waving his now-empty pistol menacingly, Adams herded a lieutenant-colonel and over 300 prisoners to the rear.

I Corps

Liggett's I Corps objective was high ground north of Thiaucourt, strategically located on the railroad from Onville. Liggett designated the veteran 2nd Division as the point of the spear.

The 2nd Division was required to move through three woods: Bois la Haie l'Evêque, the Bois du Four, and the Bois de Heiche. Thiaucourt, located along the Rupt de Mad, was the largest town in the salient after St Mihiel. The division deployed on a 1½-mile-wide frontage, with the 3rd Brigade (9th and 23rd regiments) taking the forward position, followed by the 4th Brigade (5th and 6th Marine regiments). Opposing them was the German 419th Regiment of the 77th Reserve Division. The 419th Regiment deployed its 2nd and 3rd battalions in the forward edge of the Bois la Haie l'Evêque and the Bois du Four. The German artillery's protective line was located at the back edge of the woods, supported by a *Landsturm* battalion and a pioneer company. The 1/419th was in the divisional reserve, south of Thiaucourt.

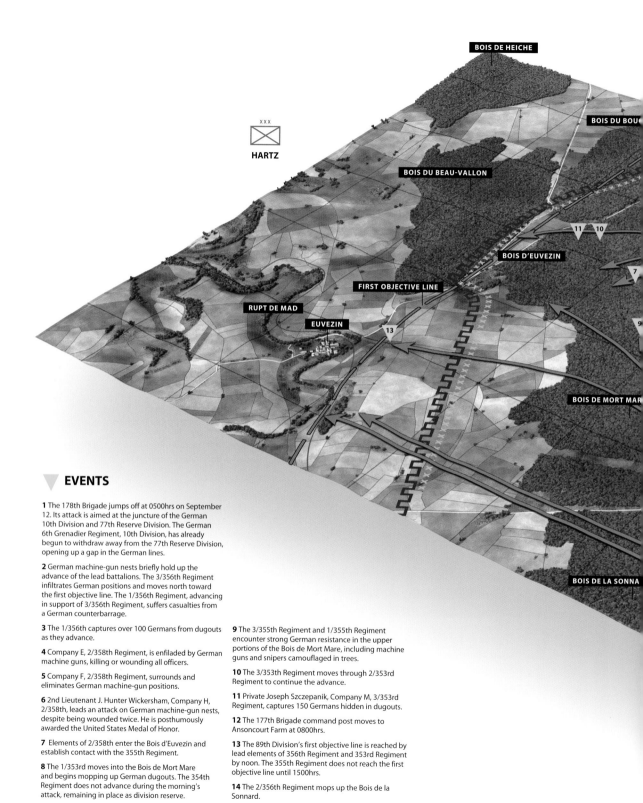

BOIS DE HEICHE

BOIS DU BOU(

XXX

HARTZ

BOIS DU BEAU-VALLON

BOIS D'EUVEZIN

11 10

7

FIRST OBJECTIVE LINE

RUPT DE MAD

EUVEZIN

9

13

BOIS DE MORT MAR

▼ EVENTS

1 The 178th Brigade jumps off at 0500hrs on September 12. Its attack is aimed at the juncture of the German 10th Division and 77th Reserve Division. The German 6th Grenadier Regiment, 10th Division, has already begun to withdraw away from the 77th Reserve Division, opening up a gap in the German lines.

2 German machine-gun nests briefly hold up the advance of the lead battalions. The 3/356th Regiment infiltrates German positions and moves north toward the first objective line. The 1/356th Regiment, advancing in support of 3/356th Regiment, suffers casualties from a German counterbarrage.

3 The 1/356th captures over 100 Germans from dugouts as they advance.

4 Company E, 2/358th Regiment, is enfiladed by German machine guns, killing or wounding all officers.

5 Company F, 2/358th Regiment, surrounds and eliminates German machine-gun positions.

6 2nd Lieutenant J. Hunter Wickersham, Company H, 2/358th, leads an attack on German machine-gun nests, despite being wounded twice. He is posthumously awarded the United States Medal of Honor.

7 Elements of 2/358th enter the Bois d'Euvezin and establish contact with the 355th Regiment.

8 The 1/353rd moves into the Bois de Mort Mare and begins mopping up German dugouts. The 354th Regiment does not advance during the morning's attack, remaining in place as division reserve.

BOIS DE LA SONNA

9 The 3/355th Regiment and 1/355th Regiment encounter strong German resistance in the upper portions of the Bois de Mort Mare, including machine guns and snipers camouflaged in trees.

10 The 3/353th Regiment moves through 2/353rd Regiment to continue the advance.

11 Private Joseph Szczepanik, Company M, 3/353rd Regiment, captures 150 Germans hidden in dugouts.

12 The 177th Brigade command post moves to Ansoncourt Farm at 0800hrs.

13 The 89th Division's first objective line is reached by lead elements of 356th Regiment and 353rd Regiment by noon. The 355th Regiment does not reach the first objective line until 1500hrs.

14 The 2/356th Regiment mops up the Bois de la Sonnard.

89TH DIVISION'S ASSAULT, SEPTEMBER 12, 1918

The Americans break through the German defenses and move into the forested terrain beyond, taking many pris

ANSONCOURT FARM

RT MESNIL FARM

LIMEY

FLIREY

BOIS DE LA VOISOIGNE

89th WRIGHT

BOIS DU JURY

GERMAN FORCES
A 6th Grenadier Regiment, 10th Reserve Division
B 257th Reserve Regiment, 77th Reserve Division

AMERICAN FORCES
1 3/356th Regiment, 89th Division
2 1/356th Regiment, 89th Division
3 2/356th Regiment, 89th Division
4 3/355th Regiment, 89th Division
5 1/355th Regiment, 89th Division
6 2/355th Regiment, 89th Division
7 Command Post, 178th Brigade, 89th Division
8 89th Division command post
9 1/354th Regiment, 89th Division
10 2/354th Regiment, 89th Division
11 3/354th Regiment, 89th Division
12 Company G, 2/353rd Regiment, 89th Division
13 Company E, 2/353rd Regiment, 89th Division
14 Company F, 2/353rd Regiment, 89th Division
15 Company H, 2/353rd Regiment, 89th Division
16 3/353rd Regiment, 89th Division
17 1/353rd Regiment, 89th Division
18 Command Post, 177th Brigade, 89th Division

The 2nd Division had received a steady supply of replacements, increasing divisional strength to 28,600, about 1,400 over its nominal strength. The experience of the 3/6th Marines was typical. On the day before the attack the battalion received 250 replacements, which were distributed throughout the companies. The men were given two extra bandoliers of rifle ammunition, extra Chauchat ammunition, and rifle grenades. Some 20 percent of each company was sent into reserve. The 3/6th was assigned a Stokes mortar platoon, a 15-man 37mm gun section, 40 pioneers for wire-cutting, and eight engineers to ensure coordination with the tanks.

Army orders established the 2nd Division's first-objective line as the Bois de Heiche. The 3/9th and 2/23rd were positioned to lead the 3rd Brigade advance, supported by a machine-gun barrage to be delivered by the 4th and 6th Machine-gun battalions. A gas-and-flame company and three companies of tanks were also attached to the 3rd Brigade.

Responding to orders for the Gorze Group to deepen its outpost zone while withdrawing the main line of resistance to the artillery's protective line, Major Nauman, commander of the 419th Regiment, issued new orders at 1830hrs on September 11. The outposts were to remain in place with machine guns but the bulk of the front-line battalions were to withdraw. These movements were well under way when the American barrage began at 0100hrs. The 2nd and 3rd battalions disintegrated under the barrage. The regimental commander and staff disappeared some time during the evening and the 1st Battalion, split into companies, made a feeble stand before collapsing under the weight of the American attack. Only 300 men of the 419th Regiment could be located on September 13.

At 0500hrs each forward company advanced in four waves, each separated by 50yds. The first two waves deployed into a thin skirmish line, with 5–10yds between each man, and the last two lines were in small columns, accompanied by the machine guns, mortars, and 37mm guns. The companies were separated by 200yd intervals and the battalions by 500yd gaps. German resistance was negligible and the 3rd Brigade moved quickly to occupy the German artillery protective line along the northern edge of Bois du Four by 0700hrs. Without pausing, the American line continued into Bois de Heiche, occupying the northern edge by 0900hrs. German defenders in the Bois la Haie l'Evêque established a loose defensive line that held up the Americans momentarily before retreating in the face of concentrated rifle fire.

American artillery pummeled the German lines while the 3rd Brigade reorganized. The 9th Regiment, which had widened its frontage during the initial advance, moved the 2/9th and 1/9th to forward positions. The 2/23rd remained the assault battalion on the left. At 1100hrs the advance continued and the German 257th Reserve Infantry Regiment attempted to make a stand on a ridge south of Thiaucourt. The German line was swept away as the 23rd Regiment passed through Thiaucourt at about noon and the 3rd Brigade reached the first-day objective by 1300hrs. The 2nd Division gathered over 3,000 prisoners, 92 guns loaded on a train, a hospital train, an ammunition train, and empty freight cars.

To the east of the 2nd Division, the 5th Division was given the objective of capturing the Bois de la Rappe. The plan then called for support battalions to advance another 2 miles, through the Bois Gérard and the heights northeast of Viéville. The 332nd Regiment, rated third class by American intelligence, faced the 5th Division. The German first line, composed of a single trench protected by bands of barbed wire, ran through open country west of the Bois de la Rappe. Beyond the first line the Bois des Saulx, Grandes Portions, and Bois St Claude formed the second combat position. The second position included two trenchlines with concrete strongpoints and reinforced dugouts.

The advance began at 0530hrs with the 10th Brigade (6th and 11th regiments) moving quickly through the wire, which they found rusted and in poor condition. A steady stream of German prisoners, including the commander of the 332nd Regiment, made their way to the rear in the wake of the American advance. Opposition stiffened briefly at the Bois des Saulx and St Claude, but by 0700hrs the 11th Infantry Regiment swept into Viéville just behind the creeping barrage. At 0930hrs the 10th Brigade drove through the Bois Gérard and occupied its first objective line. As the Americans mopped up the woods they found a large German hospital and a well-developed recreation camp, complete with a rustic beer garden and huts wired with electric lights. Working directly behind the 5th Division infantry, the 7th Engineers began clearing and rebuilding the road network to allow supplies

Infantry of the 5th Division advancing through barbed wire. American planners were concerned about the impact of large areas of German barbed wire on the initial American advance. Despite its appearance, much of the German wire turned out to be rusted and poorly maintained.

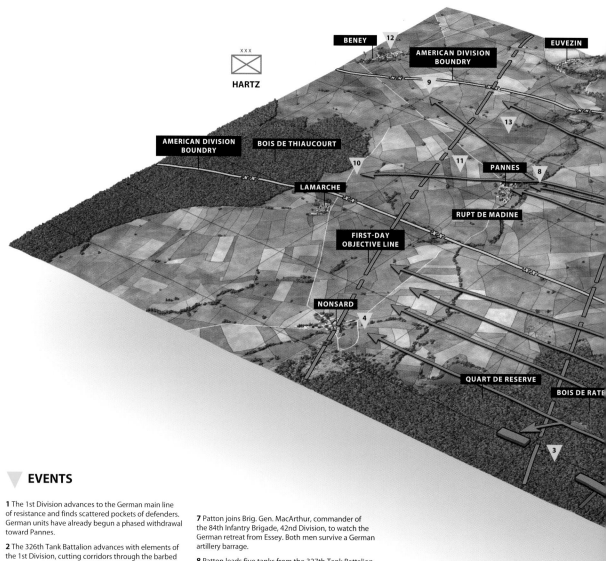

EVENTS

1 The 1st Division advances to the German main line of resistance and finds scattered pockets of defenders. German units have already begun a phased withdrawal toward Pannes.

2 The 326th Tank Battalion advances with elements of the 1st Division, cutting corridors through the barbed wire and moving toward Lahayville. One tank is lost crossing the Rupt de Mad. The 326th assists infantry from the 1st Division in attacks on the Bois de Rate.

3 The 1/18th Regiment and 2/18th Regiment are detached to guard the 1st Division's left flank.

4 The 326th Tank Battalion supports 1st Division's advance toward the first-day objective at Nonsard.

5 327th Tank Battalion supports the advance of the 42nd Division into the Bois de la Sonnard at 0800hrs. The 167th and 168th regiments encounter forward elements of the German 6th Grenadier Regiment and 47th Regiment in the northern section of the wood.

6 Lieutenant-Colonel Patton moves to a hill north of Seicheprey to observe the attacks of both tank battalions.

7 Patton joins Brig. Gen. MacArthur, commander of the 84th Infantry Brigade, 42nd Division, to watch the German retreat from Essey. Both men survive a German artillery barrage.

8 Patton leads five tanks from the 327th Tank Battalion through Essey and toward Pannes.

9 Patton is joined by scattered elements of the 83rd Brigade and advances toward Beney. Riding on the rear deck of a tank, Patton survives heavy machine-gun fire.

10 Returning to Pannes, Patton coordinates an attack with infantry from the 166th Regiment, 83rd Brigade, against the Bois de Thiaucourt.

11 At 1400hrs Patton orders the remaining tanks to return to Pannes to refuel and rearm.

12 At 1600hrs Patton's tanks join elements of the 167th Regiment in attacking Beney, capturing 16 machine guns and four 77mm artillery pieces.

13 Patton orders tanks to return to Pannes while the 167th Regiment digs in south of Beney.

AMERICAN TANK OPERATIONS, SEPTEMBER 12, 1918

Finding the German forces opposite them already in the process of withdrawing, the American 1st and 42nd div

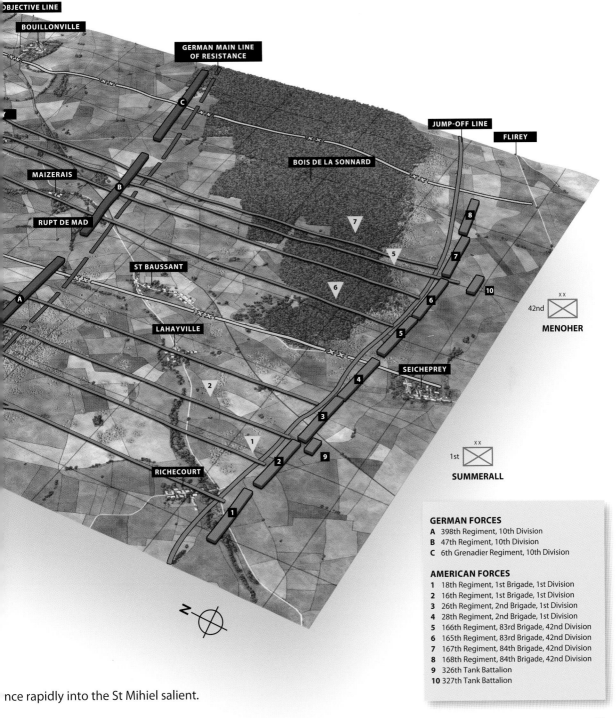

OBJECTIVE LINE

BOUILLONVILLE

GERMAN MAIN LINE
OF RESISTANCE

C

JUMP-OFF LINE

FLIREY

BOIS DE LA SONNARD

MAIZERAIS

B

8

RUPT DE MAD

7

7

5

10

A

ST BAUSSANT

6

6

42nd
XX

MENOHER

5

LAHAYVILLE

5

SEICHEPREY

2

4

1st
XX

SUMMERALL

1

3

RICHECOURT

2

9

1

N

GERMAN FORCES
A 398th Regiment, 10th Division
B 47th Regiment, 10th Division
C 6th Grenadier Regiment, 10th Division

AMERICAN FORCES
1 18th Regiment, 1st Brigade, 1st Division
2 16th Regiment, 1st Brigade, 1st Division
3 26th Regiment, 2nd Brigade, 1st Division
4 28th Regiment, 2nd Brigade, 1st Division
5 166th Regiment, 83rd Brigade, 42nd Division
6 165th Regiment, 83rd Brigade, 42nd Division
7 167th Regiment, 84th Brigade, 42nd Division
8 168th Regiment, 84th Brigade, 42nd Division
9 326th Tank Battalion
10 327th Tank Battalion

nce rapidly into the St Mihiel salient.

Advancing American troops found extensive German rest camps throughout the St Mihiel salient.

to flow to the front. Rolling kitchens and medical facilities were also moved forward and ambulance dressing stations were established at various points along the front line. The 2/60th and 2/61st from the 9th Brigade were ordered forward to support the 10th Brigade, and the advance continued toward the first-day objective. In accordance with the corps plans, the line of advance shifted to the northeast, and by 1330hrs the army objective had been secured and the troops began to dig in.

Deployed near the easternmost end of the American line along the southern face of the salient, the 90th Division had the shortest distance to move. The division was ordered to attack with the 180th Brigade on the right, making a limited advance, while the 179th Brigade on the left was expected to keep pace with the advance of the 5th Division. In the 179th Brigade sector the 357th Regiment, placed on the left, assigned the 1/357th as the assault battalion, the 2/357th as support, and placed the 3/357th in brigade reserve. The regiment was directed to move through the Bois de la Rappe and Bois St Claude and support the 5th Division's capture of Viéville. The 358th Regiment, on the right, was assigned enough frontage to deploy the 3/358th and 2/358th as assault battalions with the 1/358th in support. The 358th's objective was the Bois de Frière.

In the 180th Brigade sector the 3/359th Regiment was expected to maintain contact with the 3/358th and capture the Quart de Reserve, a 320yd^2 square of shattered trees. The 2/359th would support the attack on the Quart de Reserve while the 1/360th and 3/160th, on the far right of the divisional sector, were to remain in place facing the Bois-le-Prêtre.

As the 0500hrs jump-off time approached, the assault battalions noticed that the supporting barrage along their front was relatively thin. Prior to the attack, patrols and working parties had attempted to cut lanes through the barbed wire but had been stymied by a lack of wire-cutters. Frustrated by their inability to secure the cutters through the Army's supply system, divisional staff created a minor scandal when they attempted to purchase the wire-cutters in open markets in Toul and Nancy. By the time of the assault 400 heavy-duty wire-cutters had been procured for each brigade.

Arrayed opposite the 90th Division was the German 255th Division, rated as fourth class by American intelligence, but still able to put up stiff resistance to the American attack. On the left the 1/357th surged forward, crossing a mile of open country, through the wire and German machine-gun fire, and penetrating the Bois de la Rappe. Between the Bois de la Rappe and the Forêt des Venchères, across the road between Viéville and Vilcey-sur-Trey, was a ravine, later named Gas Alley. Machine-gun emplacements covered the steep slope leading from the road up to the edge of the Forêt des Venchères. The 1/357th struggled up the slope, swept by machine-gun fire. Officer casualties were severe but the battalion's assault brought them into the German position. Moving up in support, the 2/357th also suffered from enemy fire and found itself engaged in mopping up strongpoints bypassed by the 1/357th. The 2/357th also supported the advance of the 3/358th on their right, which was struggling to capture the Bois de Frière.

Even before the attack began, the 3/358th suffered from German artillery fire as it moved toward its jump-off positions. Major Terry Allen was wounded by shrapnel and taken to an aid station. After regaining consciousness Allen refused treatment and returned to the front, assembling ragtag groups of stragglers along the way. Allen and his men then surprised several German strongpoints bypassed by the 3/358th in its initial assault, the men fighting in close quarters with their fists after exhausting all their ammunition. Allen was wounded again in the hand-to-hand combat, losing several teeth in the process, and was later evacuated.

The 3/358th suffered from difficult terrain and German defenses. With only five out of the 12 officers in the battalion still in action, the advance bogged down. Elements of the 1/358th, coming up in support, became intermingled with the 3/358th as they struggled up the wooded valley. Captain George Danenhour, commanding Company B, and Captain Sim Souther, commanding Company M, decided to capture Vilcey-sur-Trey before nightfall, but their attack faltered several hundred yards short of the town.

Movement of supplies to the front along overcrowded roads created logistical problems throughout the St Mihiel offensive.

FIGHTING IN THE BOIS DE FRIÈRE, SEPTEMBER 12, 1918 (pp. 62–63)

The 3/358th Infantry, 90th Division, was designated the assault unit for the American attack on the morning of September 12. As they were moving forward toward their jump-off positions before dawn, the unit was caught by German counterbattery fire. Major Allen, battalion commander, was wounded and evacuated while unconscious to an aid station in the rear. Regaining his senses, Allen removed his medical tag and sought to rejoin his unit, which had already advanced through the Bois de Frière. Allen gathered a group of men separated from their units and led them forward. They discovered a group of Germans bypassed by the first wave of American troops emerging from their dugout. Allen led his men in desperate hand-to-hand combat with the Germans. After emptying his pistol and despite his wounds, Allen fought with his fists, losing several teeth and suffering another serious wound.

Allen and his men are shown engaging the Germans in the trench. On the morning of September 12, American troops wore raincoats to protect against the rain. Allen **(1)** is using his .45-caliber pistol **(2)**, which was standard issue for American officers. American tactical doctrine required the assault battalions to advance as quickly as possible toward their first objective line. Follow-on battalions were given the task of mopping up German strongpoints bypassed by the leading troops. The American early morning artillery barrage drove many German units into the protection of their dugouts **(3)** and many were passed over by the first wave of American troops. During the St Mihiel offensive several American support units engaged in desperate battles to clean out small groups of Germans scattered throughout the woods.

Allen would rise to command the American 1st Infantry Division in North Africa and Sicily in World War II. Criticized for lax discipline, Allen was relieved of his command by General Dwight Eisnhower. Allen was then assigned to command the 104th Infantry Division and he led them through the Battle of the Bulge and Germany's surrender in May 1945.

While the 3/358th was delayed in its advance, to their right the 2/358th was also hampered by German wire and machine guns. During the initial advance the battalion commander and two company commanders were wounded, leaving Captain John Simpson, of Company G, to assume command of the battalion. By 0715hrs several platoons of Company F had secured the objective line and gathered over 150 prisoners. German snipers covering the forest paths were neutralized by American "squirrel hunters" from Oklahoma and Texas; Corporal Wilbur Light won the Distinguished Service Cross for shooting six snipers out of their perches. It wasn't until 1400hrs that the remainder of the battalion came forward. The 3/358th was then ordered to secure La Poêle, a German strongpoint, and settle in for the night.

In the 180th Brigade sector 3/359th was required to slide westwards to its jump-off position. Orders were received late and not all officers were immediately informed of the move, resulting in delays in distributing ammunition and food. Combined with the darkness and rain, this resulted in several platoons being late in settling into their initial positions. The Germans defended the Quart de Reserve tenaciously. With the support of the 2/359th and despite heavy casualties, particularly among officers, companies K, L, and M occupied the Rhenane trench by 1300hrs, where they consolidated their positions. The 2/359th spent the remainder of the day securing its position and eliminating pockets of German resistance.

The role of the 82nd Division was to act as the hinge on which the I and IV Corps door would swing. While it was not expected to engage in a wholesale advance, its position was complicated. The division straddled the Moselle River, facing the German 255th Division on the west back of the Moselle together with the 84th Landwehr Brigade and 31st Landwehr Brigade. The division was expected to exert pressure on the enemy through aggressive patrols. On September 12 strong patrols were sent out to probe the German lines. A force from the 327th Regiment engaged the Germans at Bel Air Farm on the east bank and retired under strong pressure from the enemy. On the west bank of the Moselle three platoons from Company F, 328th Regiment, approached the town of Norroy, penetrating the German defenses before withdrawing. Patrols from the 325th Regiment reached Eply while probes from the 326th Regiment attacked German positions west of the Bois de la Voivrotte.

V Corps

On the western face of the salient Maj. Gen. Cameron's V Corps, led by the 26th (Yankee) Division, waited while I and IV Corps attacked the southern face. In order to further confuse the Germans, the corps was not scheduled to attack until 0800hrs. The 26th Division faced hundreds of yards of barbed wire followed by a dense system of trenches. The 51st Brigade held the right of the divisional sector. The 101st Regiment was assigned to lead the assault, followed by the 102nd Regiment in support. On the left the 52nd Brigade was formed by the 103rd Regiment and 104th Regiment abreast. The first-day objective was a ridge southeast of the Dompierre–Longeau Ferme road. Facing the 26th Division was the understrength and unmotivated 13th Landwehr Division.

Following the preliminary barrage, the men of the 26th Division moved with high anticipation into the attack. To their surprise resistance was minimal and the division was able to advance over a half-mile without serious opposition. On the far left of the 52nd Brigade sector the 104th Regiment advanced quickly, overcoming isolated pockets of resistance. To its right the 103rd Regiment encountered German machine guns in the Bois St Rémy. Flanking the German strongpoints, the 103rd Regiment shot down the gunners and continued its advance, capturing an entire enemy battalion.

On the right the 101st Regiment, deployed with two battalions in line, found itself struggling through a belt of wire measuring 90ft deep. Advancing cautiously on either side of the Grande Tranchée de Colonne, through a half-mile of shattered woods, the regiment approached the Vaux–St Rémy road and slammed into a strong line of well-constructed trenches augmented by concrete strongpoints. German artillery fire, which up to this point had been ineffective, began to fall among the American infantry. Recoiling briefly, the American infantry began to work its way around the strongpoints. Around noon the support battalions of the 102nd Regiment and 101st Machine-gun Battalion were ordered forward. After a quick reconnaissance by the 26th Division Chief of Staff, the 1/102nd was ordered to advance through the 101st and continue the attack. Colonel Hiram Bearss, commander of the 102nd Regiment, directed the 1/102nd to move forward at 1600hrs. Several men infiltrated the German line, surprising and capturing enemy machine-gun positions from the rear and unhinging the German defensive position. The 1/102nd quickly cleared the German defenses.

On the left, the 104th Regiment reported they had lost contact with the French 15th Colonial Division. The French had captured St Rémy at 2330hrs but their attack bogged down as German resistance stiffened around Amaranthe Hill. Although the 104th Regiment reported sporadic German rifle fire there was no serious danger to the open flank and the American advance continued. The V Corps staff noted the failure of the French to keep up with the 26th Division and reassigned responsibility for a portion of the front from the 15th Colonial Division to the 26th Division. The 103rd and 104th regiments continued forward into the Bois-le-Chanot. A battery of 155mm guns was captured by the 104th and both regiments extended

A German prisoner receiving medical treatment from medics of the 26th Division. Heavy rain during the night of September 11 and into the early hours of September 12 resulted in most American infantry wearing raincoats over their uniforms.

skirmish lines south toward Dommartin. Furious German machine-gun fire greeted the Americans as they worked their way up the slope toward the town. The Americans retreated back to the woods and began digging in for the night.

As the 26th Division was consolidating its positions Maj. Gen. Edwards was conferring with French 2nd Dismounted Cavalry Division commander, General Hennocque, on what steps to take next. Hennocque, whose forces had kept pace with the Americans on the right, proposed a shift to the left and an advance north toward St Maurice. Edwards agreed and directed his staff to begin preparations for the movement. On the heels of this decision V Corps commander Maj. Gen. Cameron, acting on a directive from Pershing, ordered Edwards to drive southeast to Vigneulles where they would link up with troops from the 1st Division and close the salient. Playing on longstanding tension between the National Guard officers and men of the 26th Division and the regular army leadership, Cameron told Edwards, "This is your chance, old man. Go do it … try and beat the 1st Division in the race and clean up."

War in the air

While the doughboys were shivering in mud-choked trenches enduring a night of driving rain, Colonel Billy Mitchell's airmen waited in their hangars and briefing rooms for permission to fly. Major Joseph McNarney, commander of the IV Corps Observation Group, assembled his squadron commanders. He outlined their mission for the next day and reminded them that aviation would be "a very essential part of the attack and whatever the weather the missions were to be performed as long as it was physically possible for planes to take off."

Mitchell had positioned his pursuit squadrons around the flanks of the salient along with his reconnaissance groups. The pursuit squadrons were expected to protect the observation planes and to maintain control of the air. Mitchell's plan was to coordinate observation, pursuit, and bombing missions to both support the advance of the American infantry and disrupt the German retreat. Low clouds, driving rain, and high winds conspired to unravel Mitchell's overall plan of attack. Most squadrons delayed their missions in the hope that the weather would improve. With the poor flying conditions the planes would have to fly low and it was still doubtful whether they would be able to see anything of value, considering the poor weather. Similarly, American balloons proved useless in the rain and wind. Those balloons that did rise reported poor visibility and their missions were canceled.

The French Nieuport 28, flown by American pursuit squadrons. This late variant of Nieuport's biplanes was used mainly by American pilots, notably Eddie Rickenbacker, the French having switched over to Spads.

In the early morning gloom several aircraft did get aloft and witnessed the American advance and German retreat. Observer planes reported that the Vigneulles–St Benoît road was full of men, artillery, and wagons, all in retreat. Throughout the morning small flights of observers, pursuers, and bombers managed to lift off. Once airborne, the planes experienced further frustrations in communication with ground forces. The 8th Aero Squadron found it impossible to communicate effectively with 1st Division or brigade staff. A lack of radios among ground units limited messages to handwritten notes placed in cylinders that were dropped at headquarters.

Overall, more than 50 sorties were flown by I Corps Observation Group on the first day of the offensive. On the western face of the salient V Corps Observation Group also flew some successful missions, with pilots from the 99th Aero Squadron reporting that the infantry of the 26th Division was advancing rapidly and that several villages were on fire.

The critical responsibility for penetrating the German rear areas and monitoring enemy troop movements was assigned to the First Army Observation Group. The 91st Aero Squadron, a veteran unit, which had been flying in the St Mihiel region since the spring of 1918, shouldered the bulk of the work. Although frustrated by the same weather conditions that plagued the other groups, one observer team penetrated over 50 miles into the rear of the German position and reported clear evidence of a general retreat.

German reaction

Confusion was the watchword in Army Detachment C's headquarters as information about the American attacks dribbled in. At 0700hrs it was clear that a general offensive was under way. Encouraging news filtered in at 0800hrs that a feeble attack by the French in the sector held by the 5th Landwehr Division had been repulsed. At 0930hrs the first indications that the 77th Reserve Division was in trouble reached Fuchs, with reports that retreating units had been observed in the 77th Reserve sector. In response he assigned men from the 31st and 123rd divisions to move up in support of the 77th Reserve Division and the 10th Division. The 255th Division reported that it was holding in the face of American attacks but that it had lost contact with the 77th Reserve Division on its right.

The reality on the ground was much more serious. The 77th Reserve Division had disintegrated and its neighbor the 10th Division was straining under the pressure. Unable to reach army headquarters, Gorze Group commander General Hartz ordered a counterattack by the 31st and 123rd divisions on his own initiative. The 31st Division was directed to attack through Thiaucourt and the 123rd near Viéville. Some time later communication with Conflans was restored and Hartz updated Fuchs on the deteriorating situation.

Once Fuchs and his staff overcame their initial shock at the news from the Gorze Group they began to develop a plan to restore the German front line. The 88th Division, provisionally assigned to the Combres Group, was reassigned to Hartz.

Any hope of salvaging the situation was further diminished at 1015hrs as preliminary reports suggested that the Americans had broken through the 77th Reserve Division, followed at 1050hrs with an official report from the Gorze Group that the 77th Reserve Division had been swept away and that the enemy was nearing Thiaucourt and Tautecourt Farm. Gorze also reported that there had been no signs of the expected counterattacks from the 31st and 123rd divisions. Fuchs concluded that the 10th Division's left flank had been driven back and that the Americans, nearing Thiaucourt, were threatening not only to punch a hole in the Michel Stellung but endangering the retreat of the Mihiel Group at the front of the salient.

Most troubling was news from the 35th Austrian and 13th Landwehr divisions that a strong American attack had been launched from the western face of the salient. At 1100hrs Fuchs issued orders for the Mihiel Group to begin their withdrawal, the *Loki* movement, at once. At 1110hrs General Fritz von Below, commander of the Combres Group, reported that there was heavy fighting along the Combres Heights and that St Rémy had been captured. Recognizing the American strategy of pinching off the salient with the attack from the west, Fuchs told Below that the Heights must be held.

The town of St Benoît, in which the Mihiel Group's headquarters was located, was the key to maintaining a corridor of retreat for the Group. The 65th Landwehr Regiment, 5th Landwehr Division, was directed to reinforce the defenses at St Benoît and shortly after noon the Mihiel Group began their retreat. The 5th Landwehr Division was ordered, in conjunction with the 192nd Saxon Division to its west, to maintain their forward battalions until 2000hrs and to remain in contact with American forces through aggressive patrols until the morning of September 13.

THE ADVANCE CONTINUES

With the successful advance of the morning encouraging optimism in First Army command, I Corps ordered the 1st Division to resume its attack, with the goal of the first day-two objective line. At 1335hrs the provisional squadron of the 2nd Cavalry Regiment was dispatched to Nonsard. The cavalry was ordered to proceed along the Nonsard–Vigneulles road in the hope that they could take advantage of the disorganized German retreat. Starting out at 1720hrs three troops of cavalry quickly encountered determined German resistance where the roads passed into the Bois de Nonsard. Although they were able to capture several prisoners, the cavalry was unable to advance.

Throughout the afternoon the 75mm batteries were moved forward to support the next phase of advance. At 1745hrs the 1st Division moved north from Nonsard, securing the Decauville Road through the Bois de Vigneulles and Bois de Nonsard by 1945hrs. At 2200hrs elements of the 28th Regiment

The 1st Division moving in a long column through the rolling plains of the St Mihiel salient. The terrain of the salient was characterized by open fields punctuated by large woodlands.

continued to move cautiously through the Bois de Vigneulles toward the main German line of retreat, the Vigneulles–St Benoît road. The 18th Regiment penetrated the Bois de la Belle Ozière to the west and patrols were dispatched toward Heudicourt.

Movement through the dense woods, infested with bands of Germans – some intent on surrendering, others putting up stiff resistance – was slow. Entire German companies were surrounded and captured, while the staff of a German battalion wandered into American lines searching for a predetermined rendezvous point.

Two battalions of the 42nd Division were temporarily reassigned to the 1st Division to reinforce its right flank. They were directed to be in Lamarche by 0400hrs. In addition, 6th Brigade, 3rd Division, was ordered to move forward as a 1st Division reserve.

During the afternoon of September 12 the 83rd Brigade, 42nd Division, established its headquarters in Essey. The 165th Regiment set up its headquarters in Pannes, extending patrols from the 1/165th into the southern portions of the Bois de Thiaucourt. The 2/165th was deployed in support and the 3/165th around Pannes. The 84th Brigade moved up to the east, the 168th settling in on the right of the 165th, along the southern edge of the Bois de Thiaucourt, while the 168th extended the line a half-mile northeast of Pannes. With that the 42nd Division settled down for the night.

More tanks from the 327th Tank Battalion gathered at Pannes through the course of the afternoon. The tanks were burning fuel at a much higher rate than predicted, primarily because of the mud and difficult terrain. By mid-afternoon the fuel situation was eased somewhat by a small amount moved forward on sleds pulled behind the supply tanks. An attempt to move gasoline supply trucks to Essey along the Flirey–Essey road was stopped by military police in Flirey, who refused to allow the trucks to move to Essey until the afternoon of September 13. Patton, satisfied that the 327th had achieved its objectives, started out in search of the 326th Tank Battalion in the 1st Division sector. In Nonsard he found Major Brett despondent about the small number of serviceable tanks remaining in the battalion but, more importantly, about being out of gasoline. After consoling Brett, Patton started for the rear to find more fuel.

The 89th Division Chief of Staff, Colonel C. E. Kilbourne, directed the 1/355th and 3/356th, already moving to join the 177th Brigade south of Bouillonville, to continue their advance toward the Bois de Dampvitoux. The 1/355th received the orders first and led the advance, the 3/356th on its left and the 3/353rd on its right. Moving through and beyond Bouillonville and finding no organized German opposition, the 1/355 reached its objective east of Bois de Dampvitoux at 1800hrs, while the 3/356th occupied the wood at 2000hrs and the 3/353rd moved into Xammes at midnight.

The 3rd Brigade, 2nd Division, having reached its first-day objective line at 1300hrs, paused to consolidate its positions. The 2/9th and 1/9th, deployed on the right of the brigade, had also reached the final army objective. On the left the 2/23rd pushed patrols out toward Jaulny and Xammes and by 1400hrs it had also reached the final army objective line. The 6th Marine Regiment, in support of the 23rd Regiment, maintained contact with the 89th Division on the left.

The 5th Division, having secured the army objective line at 1330hrs, sent strong patrols toward the Hindenburg Line. The division had lost contact with the 90th Division on its right, which had created a large gap. The 3/11th filled the gap, facing west. The 6th Regiment dispatched a patrol toward Rembercourt, scooping up prisoners. Later in the afternoon word was received that the 2nd Division forward elements were at Jaulny and the 5th Division realigned their left flank to conform to the 2nd Division movement. German resistance to 5th Division patrols became stronger later in the afternoon. In the early evening German reinforcements arrived between Rembercourt and La Souleuvre Ferme. The 174th Regiment, 31st Division, attacked the 6th Regiment in the Bois de Bonvaux while the 106th Regiment, 123rd Division, attacked the 11th Regiment. The German 123rd Division replaced the remnants of the 77th Reserve Division, which had lost over 1,100 men to the 5th Division.

By 1400hrs the 90th Division had fought its way to the first-day objective. In the process it had captured over 500 prisoners. While the infantry battalions began to consolidate their positions, patrols were pushed out over

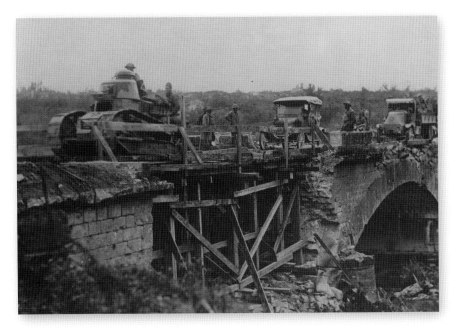

American tanks crossing a hastily repaired bridge. American engineering units were engaged throughout the offensive repairing bridges and roads in order to maintain American momentum and allow artillery and other support units to move forward.

LEFT
Three American tanks disabled because of mechanical breakdowns. Between mechanical problems and higher-than-expected fuel consumption, American tanks saw limited action late in the day on September 12.

RIGHT
German prisoners were frequently used to carry American wounded from the battlefield to aid stations.

a mile toward the German Michel Stellung, resulting in more desultory fighting. A patrol from Company A, 357th Regiment, penetrated the German defensive lines, attacking and capturing a German battery but finding itself surrounded. The patrol fought their way back to the main line, losing only one prisoner. Machine-gun battalions were moved forward to buttress the line of defense. Although the advance on September 12 had succeeded in routing the German defenses, American commanders now feared a determined German counterattack during the night.

While American reconnaissance flights observed German supply wagons clogging the roads leading north and east out of the salient they also noted the movement of German infantry toward American positions, with IV Corps Observation Group reporting "between two and three thousand enemy troops on Chambley–Dampvitoux road entering Dampvitoux." An hour later another pilot reported large numbers of enemy moving toward Thiaucourt from Waville.

STEMMING THE TIDE

Even as orders to begin the *Loki* movement directed an immediate retreat, Lieutenant-General Leuthold, the Mihiel Group commander, noted that the 5th Landwehr and 192nd Saxon divisions had repelled attacks from the II French Colonial Corps along the nose of the salient. The *Loki* movement limited a general retirement to the Schroeter zone and Leuthold issued orders in accordance with that plan. Unfortunately for Army Detachment C, the American advance had already penetrated the Schroeter zone early in the afternoon. At 1400hrs the 5th Landwehr Divison reported that Pannes and Nonsard had been captured, at which time the Mihiel Group staff determined that the "order issued by army headquarters at noon to hold the Schroeter zone had become obsolete." Fuchs, who had also hoped to reconstitute his line in the Schroeter zone in order to save large stocks of supplies, bowed to the reality of the American penetration and directed Leuthold to retire to the Michel Stellung.

About that time the headquarters of the Mihiel Group was transferred from St Benoît to Lachaussee. The veteran 10th Division, pressed back by the American 42nd and 89th divisions, protected the Mihiel Group's retreat. The German 88th Division was moving rapidly from Conflans to relieve the 5th Landwehr Division. German headquarters noted that American

tanks and infantry were reported to be advancing from Nonsard toward Heudicourt. They concluded that the reserve battalion of the 65th Landwehr Regiment, which was marching to Heudicourt, would be sufficient to drive the Americans back toward Nonsard.

After a morning of rapid advance, with the American divisions threatening to cut off the Mihiel Group, I Corps and IV Corps were vulnerable to a German counterattack. American corps and divisional plans included provisions to guard against the prospect of a German reaction. As soon as the first line of resistance was broken American artillery was sent forward to support the next phase of advance or repel a German counterattack. Through the morning of September 12 the American rate of advance had exceeded the most optimistic assumptions, resulting in uncoordinated movements. Muddy ground and destroyed roads also conspired to frustrate the movement of artillery and other support units.

In a communiqué sent at 0530hrs Fuchs stressed that "there was no mistaking the danger to the Mihiel Group from a further advance of the enemy from Beney in the direction of St Benoît." In order to blunt the American advance the 5th Landwehr Division launched a probe with the reserve battalions of the 25th and 36th Landwehr regiments from Heudicourt, with the intention of driving the American line between Pannes and Beney back toward Bouillonville. The advance of the two battalions against the flank of the American 1st Division made no impression, but was a reminder to the Americans that the Germans still had some fight left in them. Fuchs had more confidence in the anticipated counterattacks from the 31st and 123rd divisions. Poor communications, congested roads, and crumbling morale conspired to frustrate the German plan. Owing to the haphazard arrival of both divisions, neither attack materialized as intended. The 31st Division joined the remnants of the left wing of the 10th Division around Xammes and then extended its line westward to Jaulny. The 123rd Division deployed farther west, linking up with the 255th Division, and prepared to attack toward Viéville.

Rather than launch a coordinated counterattack, both divisions directed limited attacks late in the afternoon. The 1/9th, 2nd Division, occupied the ground south of Jaulny in the late afternoon and pushed out patrols into the town, capturing over 100 Germans before retiring. At 1700hrs the Germans subjected the 1/9th to machine-gun and artillery fire, causing it to pull back. As the Germans advanced out of Jaulny, American machine-gun fire, coupled with an artillery barrage, broke up the attack and by 1900hrs the front was

LEFT
Despite losing large numbers of artillery pieces during the initial American attack, German reinforcements were deployed on September 13. Thiaucourt was subjected to repeated German artillery attacks.

RIGHT
Although surprised by the American attack, the Germans were able to destroy some strategic assests, such as this railroad bridge.

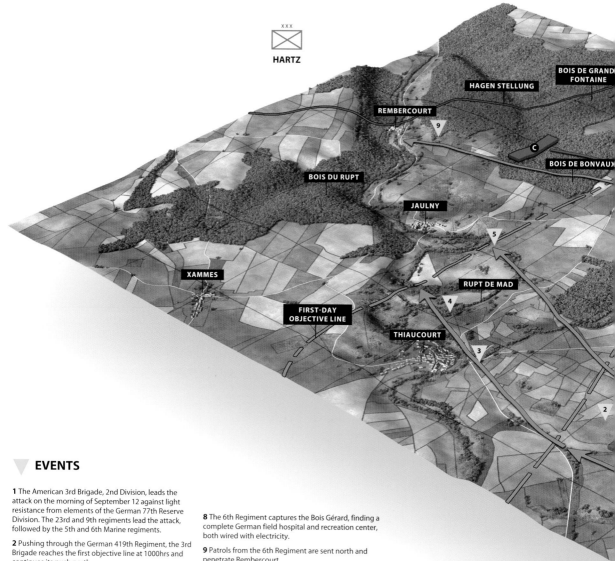

Map labels:
HARTZ
HAGEN STELLUNG
BOIS DE GRAND FONTAINE
REMBERCOURT
BOIS DE BONVAUX
BOIS DU RUPT
JAULNY
XAMMES
RUPT DE MAD
FIRST-DAY OBJECTIVE LINE
THIAUCOURT

EVENTS

1 The American 3rd Brigade, 2nd Division, leads the attack on the morning of September 12 against light resistance from elements of the German 77th Reserve Division. The 23rd and 9th regiments lead the attack, followed by the 5th and 6th Marine regiments.

2 Pushing through the German 419th Regiment, the 3rd Brigade reaches the first objective line at 1000hrs and continues its push north.

3 The 23rd Regiment captures Thiaucourt at noon, September 12.

4 The 23rd Regiment continues its advance and reaches the first-day objective line at 1430hrs.

5 The 9th Regiment advances east of Thiaucourt to the first-day objective line, where it digs in for the day.

6 The 6th and 11th regiments lead the advance of the 5th Division. Both regiments advance through the woods, leaving the work of mopping up the German defenders to the 60th and 61st regiments.

7 The 11th Regiment captures Viéville, defended by the German 332nd Regiment.

8 The 6th Regiment captures the Bois Gérard, finding a complete German field hospital and recreation center, both wired with electricity.

9 Patrols from the 6th Regiment are sent north and penetrate Rembercourt.

10 The 11th Regiment is ordered to move into open ground near the Bois Hanido and secure the first-day objective line.

11 The German 77th Reserve Division, having been shattered by the American attack, is ordered to retire in the afternoon, replaced by the 123rd Saxon and 31st divisions.

12 The German 174th Regiment, 31st Division, attacks the 6th Regiment in the Bois Gérard in the early evening but is driven off.

13 The German 106th Reserve Regiment, 123rd Saxon Division, launches a series of attacks out of the Bois Hanido against the 11th Regiment, without success.

OPERATIONS OF THE 2ND AND 5TH DIVISIONS, SEPTEMBER 12, 1918

The Americans advance to their objective lines, beating off weak German counterattacks.

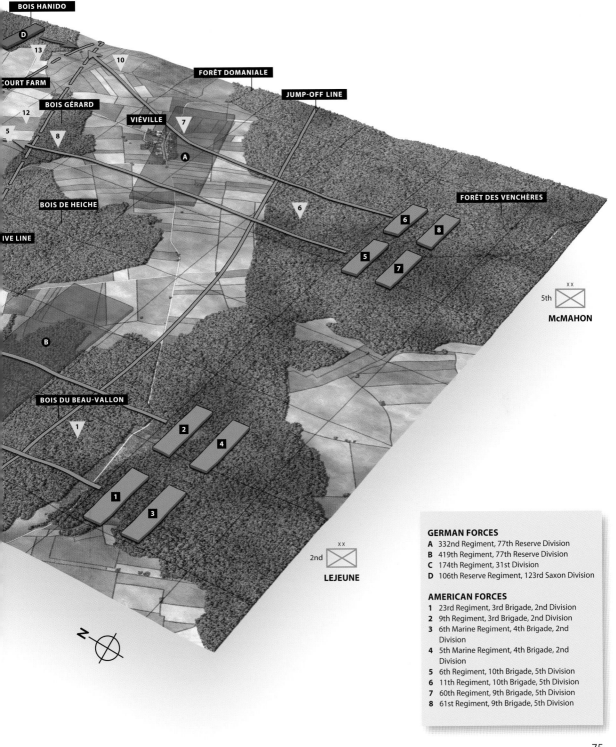

BOIS HANIDO

D

13

10

COURT FARM

FORÊT DOMANIALE

JUMP-OFF LINE

BOIS GÉRARD

12

VIÉVILLE

7

5

8

A

BOIS DE HEICHE

6

FORÊT DES VENCHÈRES

IVE LINE

6

8

5

7

5th

McMAHON

B

BOIS DU BEAU-VALLON

1

2

4

1

3

2nd

LEJEUNE

GERMAN FORCES
A 332nd Regiment, 77th Reserve Division
B 419th Regiment, 77th Reserve Division
C 174th Regiment, 31st Division
D 106th Reserve Regiment, 123rd Saxon Division

AMERICAN FORCES
1 23rd Regiment, 3rd Brigade, 2nd Division
2 9th Regiment, 3rd Brigade, 2nd Division
3 6th Marine Regiment, 4th Brigade, 2nd Division
4 5th Marine Regiment, 4th Brigade, 2nd Division
5 6th Regiment, 10th Brigade, 5th Division
6 11th Regiment, 10th Brigade, 5th Division
7 60th Regiment, 9th Brigade, 5th Division
8 61st Regiment, 9th Brigade, 5th Division

quiet. Single regimental attacks from both the 123rd and 31st divisions struck forward elements of the 5th Division late in the afternoon without effect. Although Fuchs was unable to retake lost ground or seriously threaten the American advance, he had plugged the hole created by the disintegration of the 77th Reserve Division and continued to hold a line of retreat through Heudicourt, Vigneulles, St Benoît, and Dampvitoux. The 88th Division, which had originally been dispatched to replace the 5th Landwehr Division, was redirected to the Lahayville sector to reinforce the remnants of the 10th Division and protect the right flank of the Gorze Group.

The Combres Group resisted any deep penetrations of its zone throughout most of the day. The Austrian 35th Division retired in good order to its artillery line and the 13th Landwehr Division blunted the advance of the 15th Colonial Division, which in turn slowed the advance of the 26th Division. Austrian 35th Division commander Major-General Podhoransky was confident enough in the strength of this position that he did not authorize a further retirement until 1600hrs. At 1700hrs the Combres Group commander, General Below, ordered the full retreat of the 35th Division and 13th Landwehr Divison to the Michel Stellung.

RACE TO VIGNEULLES

Despite increased German aggressiveness late in the day, Pershing and his staff were convinced that they were in full retreat. In their assessment the Americans recognized that a window of opportunity had opened. In order to escape the closing jaws of the American attack the Germans needed to withdraw the bulk of their forces during the night. The deeper-than-anticipated penetrations of the American forces offered the possibility that those jaws could be snapped shut before the Germans could escape. Late in the afternoon Pershing abandoned the carefully prepared plans and timetables, which were now obsolete, and began to improvise. At 1700hrs Pershing called V Corps commander Maj.-Gen. Cameron and directed him to detach at least one regiment and march southeast toward Vigneulles. At the same time Pershing ordered Maj. Gen. Dickman to throw the 1st Division at Vigneulles from the south.

The 26th Division commander, Maj. Gen. Edwards, received Pershing's order at 1930hrs and immediately set the advance in motion. Until Pershing called, Edwards had been reorienting his division to the northeast to assist the 15th Colonial Division in clearing the Heights of the Meuse. Edwards notified 51st Brigade commander Brigadier-General George Shelton just after 2000hrs of the change of plans and Shelton designated the 1/102nd to lead the advance. Following the lead battalion, the 102nd and 101st machine-gun battalions would march in support, followed in turn by the 2/102nd and 3/102nd. Shelton considered assigning a field-artillery regiment to the column, but the difficulty of moving guns in darkness over unknown terrain made him decide to send the infantry without artillery support.

Shelton's plan, submitted to 1/102nd staff at 2100hrs, proposed marching down the Grande Tranchée roadway, built by Louis XVI to provide improved access to his chateau at Hattonchâtel, through the woods to Vigneulles. The 1/102nd commander, Col. Bearss, a cigar-smoking Marine officer, assembled his officers and announced that this was a race against the 1st Division. He also told them he planned to march directly down the road, without throwing out flanking parties to protect his column from ambush. Bearss believed the

During the night march to Vigneulles, Col. Bearss and the 102nd Regiment surprised a column of German trucks parked along the road and took them prisoner.

Germans to be on the run and unable to offer organized resistance. Darkness would work in his favor, sheltering his men as they worked their way down the Grande Tranchée to Vigneulles.

Edwards directed his other brigade, led by Brigadier-General Eli Cole, to advance by roads east of Bearss' brigade to St Maurice. The orders to Cole were late and by the time his battalion and company commanders were informed it was after 0400hrs. St Maurice was alight with burning ammunition and supplies when the first American patrols arrived around dawn to find the Germans gone.

The 1/102nd marched steadily along the Grande Tranchée, which had been used by the Germans as a main supply artery and kept in good shape. To ensure surprise Bearss ordered his men to empty their rifles and fix bayonets. Any opposition was to be met with cold steel. Throughout the march the Americans heard movement along either side of the road, which they suspected was the sound of groups of Germans trying to escape. Coming up on a line of trucks along the side of the road, Bearss' men surprised the sleeping drivers and took them prisoner. Farther on, the Americans captured several staff officers and their car and then surprised another group, who were loading trucks with ammunition. A few shots scattered the German crews and the march continued. Just after midnight the column found Hattonchâtel in flames and to the east the Woëvre Plain alight with burning villages and supply dumps. Collecting German stragglers along the way, the 1/102nd continued toward Vigneulles. At 0230hrs on September 13 the Americans entered Vigneulles and quickly spread out.

As they moved to secure the town a German column appeared, marching from the opposite direction. Without hesitating, Bearss approached the head of the column and demanded their surrender. When the German commanding officer hesitated, Bearss laid him out with a right to the jaw and the men in the column threw up their hands. As they were corralling the prisoners a German wagon train, carrying a machine-gun battalion, appeared and suffered the same fate.

As the town was mopped up, reinforced patrols were sent south to Heudicourt and southwest to Creue, where additional prisoners were taken. Having won the race, Bearss was content to wait for the 1st Division to show up.

Assault of the 90th Division, 0500hrs, September 12, 1918

1. Despite stiff initial German resistance, the 1/357th captures the first trenchline and advances towards its first-day objective.
2. The 1/357th reaches its first-day objective by 1000hrs.
3. The 3/358th is caught in a German counterbarrage and its advance is delayed. Major Terry Allen is wounded.
4. The 3/358th fights through the first trenchline and makes slow progress through the Bois de Friere.
5. The 2/357th follows the 1/357th, mopping up German strongpoints and filling the gap created by the delay of the 3/358th.
6. The 2/357th occupies Claude trench.
7. The 2/358th suffers severe casualties during its initial assault on the first German trench, struggling through a wide belt of barbed wire under intense machine-gun fire.
8. Company F, 2/358th, captures 165 prisoners in the Bois de Friere.
9. The 1/358th advances in support. Company C, 1/358th, joins elements of Company M, 3/358th. They attempt to capture Vilcey-sur-Trey but are driven back.
10. Companies G and H, 2/358th, capture German strongpoints at La Poele trench.
11. The 3/359th captures and occupies Rhenane trench.
12. The 1/360th and the 3/360th push forward with little German opposition.

|||||||||||	German entrenchment
• • • • • •	First-day objective line
– – –	Jump-off line, September 12, 1918
←	Allied advances

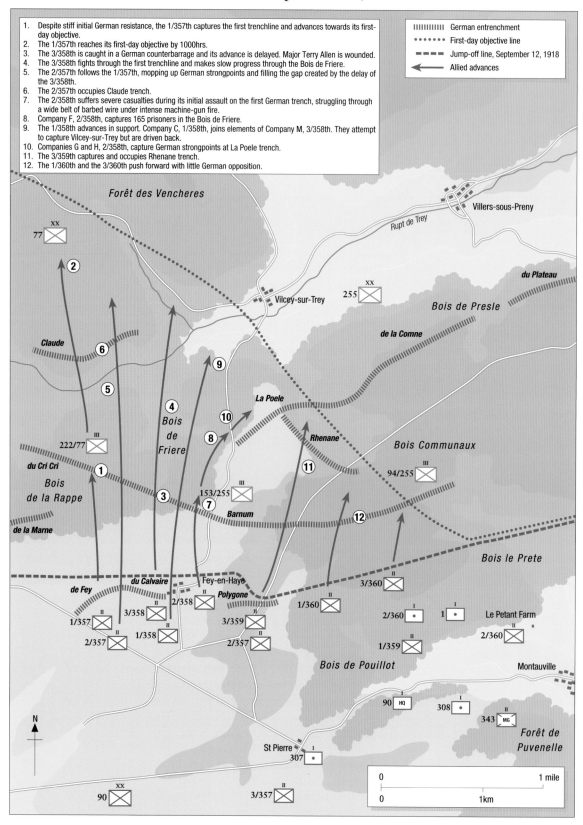

Unavoidable delays in transmitting orders from corps to division and then to brigade and regiment resulted in the 1st Division beginning its advance 45 minutes after Bearss had occupied Vigneulles. Starting out in pouring rain at 0315hrs, men from the 28th Regiment captured several German prisoners before running into two doughboys coming from the direction of Vigneulles. After some initial confusion, word went out to First Army command that Vigneulles was in American hands.

Throughout the night a jittery American staff at both army and corps levels fretted over the expected German counterattack. During the night several Germans from the 31st Division were captured and confirmed the deployment in the Michel Stellung.

Rumors of a German counterattack consumed the I Corps staff around midnight. A wireless message from the 2nd Division requesting immediate artillery support for the 26th Regiment, which was said to be under attack, resulted in the release of a brigade of the 78th Division to support the 2nd Division and a furious artillery barrage along the 26th Regiment's front. General Lejeune, 2nd Division commander, was puzzled by the message. As far as he knew the division was not under attack and passed that information back to corps staff. Because of broken communications wires and German jamming of the wireless radios, Lejeune's message was never received. The 2nd Division Chief of Staff responded later in the morning, "What goddamned fool sent the report about counterattack and falling back? If I can find the son-of-a-bitch I'm going to shoot him… The 2nd Division is to hold the Army objective as laid down and defined. That ends it."

SEPTEMBER 13

As word of the capture of Vigneulles greeted Pershing on the morning of his 58th birthday, First Army staff took stock of the first day's success and looked forward to the next steps. Now that the western portion of the salient had been cut off and all American units were roughly 24 hours ahead of schedule the objective was to wheel the entire line to the northeast. I Corps still needed to capture the Bois-le-Prêtre and the portion of the 82nd Division on the east bank of the Moselle would advance to cover the right flank. First Army orders for September 13 were simple and direct: "The attack will continue tomorrow with a view to completing the hostile defeat and gathering the booty."

While the Americans prepared to advance to the Michel Stellung, General Gallwitz also reviewed the aftermath of the American attack. Although he and General Fuchs had been surprised by the timing of the American assault they had salvaged what they could. Leuthold had been able to rebuff the French probes and had responded quickly to the order to withdraw, bringing the 5th Landwehr and 192nd Saxon divisions out of the salient just ahead of the American capture of Vigneulles. Similarly, the Combres Group had stymied the advance of the American V Corps and French II Colonial Corps throughout most of the day and had successfully withdrawn under pressure, losing only 1,100 men and three guns. Only the collapse of the 77th Reserve Division and the mauling of the veteran 10th Division in the Gorze Group had threatened to turn a tactical defeat into a catastrophe.

Gallwitz's bigger concern was what would happen next. He was convinced that the larger American plan was to push through the Michel Stellung and toward Metz. He recognized that while the Michel Stellung was stronger than the exposed deployments in the former salient, it was vulnerable to a sustained attack. Ludendorff shared Gallwitz's concerns, and as news of the extent of the defeat became known his staff noticed that his usual calm reserve seemed shaken, despite his optimistic pronouncements.

With limited reserves available in the near term, Gallwitz could only direct his troops already in the Michel Stellung to redouble their efforts to reinforce their defenses and wait for the next American move.

Throughout the morning of September 13 more units of the 1st Division drifted north toward Vigneulles. With word slow to circulate that the 26th Division had secured the town, in the early morning several potentially unfortunate incidents were averted only when 1st Division battalion commanders realized that the men milling around the town were doughboys. The movement of the 26th Division coupled with the advance of the 42nd Division had effectively pinched out the 1st Division, which was directed to prepare to be moved to the Meuse–Argonne front.

With the 1st Division already engaged in securing its juncture with the 26th Division at Vigneulles, the 42nd Division prepared to resume its advance at 0600hrs on September 13. Pivoting toward the northeast to conform to the new army objectives, the 84th Brigade, deployed on the right, was ordered to move toward Haumont. The 83rd Brigade on the left focused its attention on capturing St Benoît. At 0630hrs 15 tanks from the 327th Tank Battalion reported to Brig. Gen. MacArthur. He directed them to remain in cover in reserve, where he could call on them if needed. The 84th Brigade advanced rapidly, bypassing the Bois de Thiaucourt and Bois de Beney. The 3/168th responded to a report of a large enemy troop concentration near Louisville Farm as it moved through the Bois de Dampvitoux. Leading two platoons forward, Major Claude Stanley found only a small rearguard, which was captured after a brief firefight. On the left the 1/165th led the 83rd Brigade advance toward St Benoît. Finding that the Germans had abandoned the town during the night, the 165th Regiment occupied the former headquarters of the Mihiel Group, collecting large amounts of supplies and small bodies of stragglers. The rolling kitchens arrived in St Benoît at 1600hrs and MacArthur established his brigade headquarters in an abandoned chateau.

About mid-morning additional gasoline supplies arrived in Pannes, allowing the 327th Tank Battalion to provide MacArthur with a reserve of 35 tanks in St Benoît. Although Captain Compton was ordered to move his tanks forward at 2330hrs in response to rumors of an enemy counterattack, nothing materialized and the 327th Tank Battalion spent the next day refitting and beginning its journey back to its assembly point in the Bois de la Hazelle. In the 1st Division sector the 326th Tank Battalion also received gasoline supplies later in the afternoon, allowing Major Brett to get a force of 50 tanks to Vigneulles by midnight.

To the right of the 42nd Division the 89th had reported that the 177th Brigade had arrived at the army objective line by 2200hrs. Elements of the 178th Brigade, 3/353rd, entered Xammes and found fires still burning in the military kitchens and huge kettles of hot food, abandoned by the Germans in their haste. All around were scattered the grotesque remains of horses and men, killed by the American artillery barrage. About midnight the 177th Brigade commander Brigadier-General Frank Winn received an urgent message from division headquarters that several thousand Germans were massing at Mon Plaisir Farm, south of Charey, for an attack in the direction of Thiaucourt. During the night, the 354th Regiment was released from

division reserve and moved to Bouillonville and then in the early morning deployed into the line between the 353rd and 355th regiments. Winn moved his headquarters into Bouillonville at 0300hrs on September 13 and continued to monitor developments until dawn.

The 178th Brigade headquarters was established for the night at Euvezin, well back from the front. During the day the 178th Brigade headquarters moved to Beney. The 89th Division spent most of September 13 dodging German artillery and digging in. Losses to artillery fire were severe and mounted when orders for the men to remain in their holes were largely ignored. Division commander Maj. Gen. Wright visited Brigadier-General Thomas Hanson at Euvezin during the morning and then Brigadier-General Winn at Bouillonville. While at Bouillonville, Wright told Winn to make extra efforts to maintain contact with Brigadier-General Hanson Ely's 3rd Brigade, 2nd Division, on his right. Wright had been told earlier that Ely had refused to extend his left flank to Xammes. During his movement through the 89th Division's sector Wright noted many stragglers from the 89th, 42nd, and 2nd divisions in the German dugouts scattered through the woods with no intention of returning to their units. Wright requested a cavalry troop from IV Corps to help persuade these men to rejoin their commands.

Both the 2nd and 5th divisions spent September 13 consolidating their positions and sending patrols forward to probe the Michel Stellung. Artillery was brought up over the shell-pocketed terrain. By 1100hrs the 2nd Division reported that their light artillery was in place to support their lines and that the heavier batteries were expected later in the evening. Trench-mortar personnel were assigned to man captured German artillery and fire indiscriminately toward the German lines. A 2nd Division probe toward Mon Plaisir Farm resulted in a small yet bloody repulse. During the evening the 4th Brigade, composed of the 5th and 6th Marine regiments, replaced the 3rd Brigade, completing the relief at 0400hrs on September 14.

The 5th Division also focused its energies on reorganizing. At 1300hrs on September 13, 5th Division patrols reported a possible German counterattack by two battalions of the 106th Reserve Regiment, 123rd Saxon Division, which were assembling in the Bois Hanido. The 5th Division artillery attempted to disrupt the enemy concentrations at 1530hrs, but ammunition shortages prevented an effective barrage. German artillery increased in tempo throughout the afternoon, focusing on the 11th Regiment deployed in the Bois Gérard. German infantry advanced at 1650hrs from the Bois Hanido and Bois de Bonvaux against the Bois Gérard. The Germans also launched an

LEFT
The 102nd Regiment captured a German command group riding in this car as they marched to Vigneulles.

RIGHT
The town of Vigneulles seen from Hattonchâtel. The 102nd Regiment reached Hattonchâtel about midnight and looked out over Vigneulles and the burning villages farther beyond.

Night march of the 26th Division

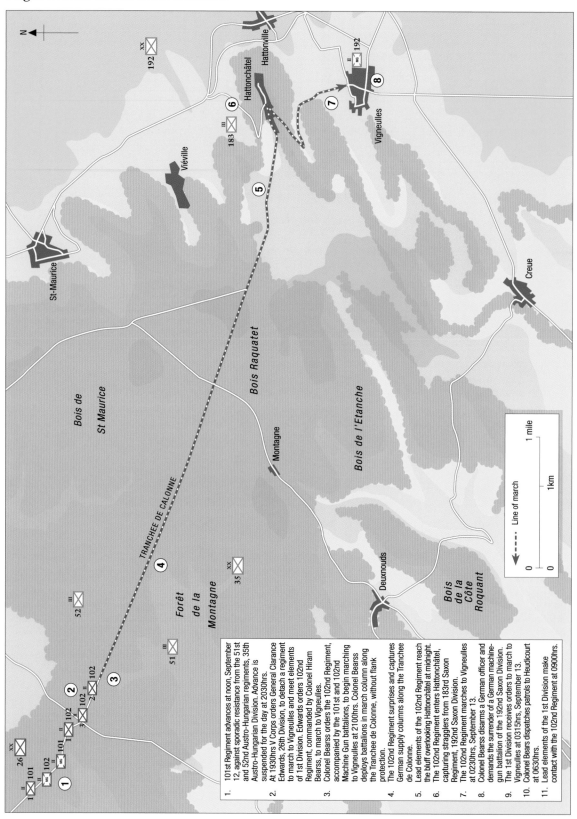

1. 101st Regiment advances at noon, September 12, against sporadic resistance from the 51st and 52nd Austro-Hungarian regiments, 35th Austro-Hungarian Division. Advance is suspended for the day at 2030hrs.

2. At 1930hrs V Corps orders General Clarance Edwards, 26th Division, to detach a regiment to march to Vigneulles and meet elements of 1st Division. Edwards orders 102nd Regiment, commanded by Colonel Hiram Bearss, to march to Vigneulles.

3. Colonel Bearss orders the 102nd Regiment, accompanied by the 101st and 102nd Machine Gun battalions, to begin marching to Vigneulles at 2100hrs. Colonel Bearss deploys battalions in march column along the Tranchee de Colonne, without flank protection.

4. The 102nd Regiment surprises and captures German supply columns along the Tranchee de Colonne.

5. Lead elements of the 102nd Regiment reach the bluff overlooking Hattonchâtel at midnight.

6. The 102nd Regiment enters Hattonchâtel, capturing stragglers from 183rd Saxon Regiment, 192nd Saxon Division.

7. The 102nd Regiment marches to Vigneulles at 0230hrs, September 13.

8. Colonel Bearss disarms a German officer and demands the surrender of a German machine-gun battalion of the 192nd Saxon Division.

9. The 1st Division receives orders to march to Vigneulles at 0315hrs, September 13.

10. Colonel Bears dispatches patrols to Heudicourt at 0630hrs.

11. Lead elements of the 1st Division make contact with the 102nd Regiment at 0900hrs.

attack from the Forêt des Venchères along the eastern flank against the 15th Machine-gun Battalion. By 2000hrs the Germans had gained a small foothold in the northeast corner of the Bois Gérard but reinforcements from the 6th Regiment helped restore the situation and by 2200hrs the attack had been repulsed all along the line.

The 90th Division spent the night of September 12–13 bringing up artillery and machine-gun battalions in preparation for an anticipated German counterattack. In compliance with the army directive to extend patrols to probe the Michel Stellung, the 3/357th set out during the morning of September 13. Working northward through the Forêt des Venchères, the doughboys encountered lead elements of the 106th Reserve Regiment, 123rd Saxon Division, moving south. The 106th Reserve Regiment had started from Onville at 0400hrs, moving through the La Grange-en-Haye Farm at 0545hrs with the objective of securing a crossroads southwest of Preney and protecting a narrow-gauge railroad that ran through St Marie Farm. The 106th Reserve Regiment was to screen the movement of the remainder of the Saxon 123rd Division, which was to launch an attack at 1100hrs against Viéville in the 5th Division sector. Elements of the 106th Reserve Regiment and the 3/357th engaged in a bitter fight throughout most of the day in the Forêt des Venchères, which ended with both sides digging in and continuing their fight into the night. The attack of the 3/257th delayed but did not stop the attack of the 123rd Saxon Division in the direction of Viéville. Later in the afternoon the Germans attacked the 5th Division in the area of the Bois Gérard.

The 1/358th also moved north early in the morning of September 13, moving without opposition through the Vilcey-sur-Trey valley and into the Forêt des Venchères. By nightfall the battalion had probed to the St Marie valley, where they established a line of defense.

The 360th Regiment was assigned the task of clearing the Bois-le-Prêtre and the Norroy quarries to the north. The 2/360th and 3/360th led the attack, jumping off at 0700hrs. Both battalions moved directly through the Bois-le-Prêtre, engaged in a day-long effort to eliminate scattered German concrete strongpoints and machine-gun nests. By 1700hrs they had secured the quarries and the 3/360th extended patrols into Norroy, which they found abandoned. An outpost was established northeast of Norroy at the Croix de Vandières, in the 82nd Division sector. The 360th found large quantities of supplies in Norroy, including medical supplies and ammunition. They also found elegant dining rooms and fully furnished recreation rooms abandoned by the Germans. The 3/360th also sent patrols into the Bois-le-Pesle and with the 2/360th they occupied the Bois-le-Pesle by nightfall.

LEFT
American tanks were ordered to St Benoît on September 13 to support Brig. Gen. MacArthur's brigade against an anticipated German counterattack.

RIGHT
This section of German trench, defended by an MG08/15, was hastily abandoned during the German retreat.

A battery of American 155mm guns deployed to support the American attack.

The 82nd Division, operating to the east of the 90th Division, was directed to protect the right flank of the 90th Division during the afternoon of September 13. The 2/328th, along with elements of the 321st Machine-gun battalion, 328th Stokes Mortar Battalion, and divisional engineers jumped off after learning that the 90th Division had pushed into the Bois-le-Prêtre and were approaching Norroy from the southwest. The 68th Landwehr Regiment, 255th Division, abandoned Norroy in the face of the advance of the 82nd and 90th divisions.

On the east bank of the Moselle the 82nd Division was ordered to undertake a strong raid against Bel Air Farm, to gather intelligence and disrupt any German attempt to move reserves to the west. Several companies from the 327th Regiment attacked at 1800hrs behind an artillery barrage and smokescreen. The Americans secured Bel Air Farm and penetrated Bois de la Tête d'Or, taking several prisoners. During the American withdrawal the Germans launched a counterattack, which was broken up by Company B, 321st Machine-gun Battalion.

The success of the advance of the 328th Regiment had put them several miles north of the remainder of the division, with their right flank protected by nothing more than the Moselle, which was fordable in several locations. In addition, the regiment was subject to German artillery fire from guns positioned east of the river.

After their successful march to Vigneulles the 51st Brigade, 26th Division, spent the morning of September 13 consolidating their hold on the town. As the 51st Brigade was advancing to Vigneulles farther to the northeast, the 52nd Brigade had extended patrols into St Maurice around daybreak. Later in the morning the bulk of the brigade moved slowly through Dommartin and crested the ridge overlooking St Maurice at noon.

Back in Vigneulles, the 51st Brigade was subjected to a raid by American bombers, unaware that the doughboys had secured the town, injuring 35 men. The brigade sent several patrols in search of German artillery, deployed in the woods to the east of Vigneulles, which was sporadically shelling the town and the 1st Division to the south. The amount of supplies in Vigneulles was beyond the ability of military police to secure and included beer and mineral water, canned provisions, clothes, and weapons of every description. Also in abundance were German and Austrian stragglers, both groups and individuals, wandering the battlefield waiting to be taken into custody by the Americans. Throughout the day the 26th Division pushed northeast from Vigneulles, occupying Herbeuville and Hannonville. Patrols were extended to Saulx, Marchéville, and Damvillers, which were found to be deserted. During the afternoon the 2nd French Dismounted Cavalry Division began to relieve the 26th Division around Vigneulles.

General Fuchs was both relieved and worried as the Americans remained largely inactive throughout September 13. Despite having avoided a wholesale disaster by withdrawing the bulk of his command on September 12, Fuchs was still apprehensive about future American intentions. So too was the German high command. Losses in men, guns, and *matériel* had been high and Hindenburg questioned the rapid withdrawal of the Mihiel Group and why nothing had been done to buttress the 77th Reserve Division.

Pershing was well pleased with the execution of his offensive and joined General Pétain in the town of St Mihiel during the afternoon. During their meeting Pershing convinced Pétain that there was justification to adjusting the line to be held by the 5th, 90th, and 82nd divisions. The disorganization of the German defenders north of the Rupt de Mad suggested that the line should be established between Pagny-sur-Moselle and Jaulny. Pétain agreed, stating that, "It will be desirable, naturally, to advance equally the outpost line on this part of the front, to a depth which the General commanding the American Army will determine."

SEPTEMBER 14

September 14 dawned clear and sunny and the First US Army now extended over 26 miles from Norroy astride the Moselle River, through Rembercourt and St Benoît to Marchéville. While Pershing and his staff looked wistfully toward Metz and wondered about the possibilities, others were openly challenging conventional orthodoxy. MacArthur, on his own initiative, accompanied by an aide, had made his way across the Michel Stellung during the night of September 13–14. MacArthur returned, having seen Metz in the distance and convinced that the German defenses were mere shells that would crack under the slightest pressure. He argued in forceful terms that if allowed to attack, his brigade would be in Metz by nightfall. His arguments made no impression on 42nd Division commander Major-General Charles Menoher, and MacArthur was told that his brigade would stay where it was.

While not completely understanding the lack of aggressive American actions, both Fuchs and Gallwitz were grateful for another day's respite from the anticipated attack. Both the Fifth Army and Army Detachment C were reinforced with three divisions each. Gallwitz demanded that both armies hold the Michel Stellung and went as far as lecturing his men not to fear the American "tanks ... and even those which have broken through are not

AMERICAN TANKS AT JONVILLE, SEPTEMBER 14, 1918 (pp. 86–87)

On September 14 at 1330hrs Patton dispatched Lt. McClure with three FT-17 Renault tanks **(1)** from the 326th Tank Battalion to lead a patrol to Woël. After confirming that the village was unoccupied, McClure's patrol was attacked by a battalion of German infantry **(2)**, accompanied by a battery of 77mm guns **(3)**. McClure dispatched a messenger to Patton, who responded by sending five additional tanks to reinforce McClure's patrol. At 0230hrs the eight American tanks engaged in a running battle with the Germans, driving them back nearly 4 miles to the village of Jonville. Although they briefly captured four 77mm guns, German resistance and a lack of infantry support forced the Americans to abandon the guns and retire, just as German 150mm artillery blanketed the area. Two American tanks that suffered mechanical problems were towed back to the battalion headquarters and the entire American force retired to St Maurice.

American tank forces used the FT-17 Renault tank extensively during the St Mihiel offensive and later in the Meuse–Argonne fighting. During the St Mihiel offensive American tank units were assigned to support infantry units and attack German machine-gun positions. Despite mechanical problems and fuel shortages, American tanks proved highly effective in the opening days of the attack. However, the experience of the advance on Jonville taught American tank commanders how vulnerable they were without effective infantry support.

dangerous if calm and presence of mind are preserved." Despite his forthright directive he added ominously, "If contrary to expectations the enemy succeeds in penetrating on the interior flanks and the situation cannot be restored by counterattack, the Volker Stellung there or the Orne will be held in any case."

Early on September 14 Patton met with Major Brett, 326th Tank Battalion, who was carrying out a desperate search for the infantry of the 1st Division. Having a vague idea of where the front was, Patton directed Brett to move his unit through St Maurice and toward Woël. At 0900hrs Patton caught up with Brett's column just over a mile west of Woël. Brett reported that he had still not made contact with American infantry. Considering his options, Patton waved down a passing American staff car and First Army Intelligence Officer Brigadier-General Dennis Nolan told Patton that the Germans had evacuated Woël, which was now held by a platoon of French infantry. Frustrated, Patton fired off messages to Rockenbach, IV Corps, and the 1st Division headquarters asking for instructions. Patton also sent out a patrol on horseback. At noon Patton dispatched Lieutenant Edwin McClure to Woël with a patrol of three tanks, accompanied by infantry. McClure reported no enemy but as they began their return they were attacked by a German infantry battalion with a battery of 77mm guns. Patton dispatched a group of five tanks to assist McClure and without infantry support Patton's eight tanks engaged in a running battle, which witnessed the Americans driving the Germans back to Jonville, destroying a dozen machine guns and capturing four 77mm guns. McClure's group was shelled as they tried to attach the captured guns to the tanks. The guns were disabled and abandoned, and two tanks were towed back after breaking down. The German artillery followed McClure back to the main force and Patton ordered a retirement to St Maurice. By 2100hrs Patton was ordered to bring the 326th Tank Battalion back to meet the 327th Tank Battalion.

With Pétain's permission to readjust his line as he saw fit, Pershing ordered Liggett's I Corps to push up the Michel Stellung. In the 1st Division sector the 4th Brigade, which had relieved the 3rd Brigade during the early morning, dispatched patrols from the 5th and 6th Marine regiments at dawn. Later in the day General Lejeune ordered additional patrols to be sent out at 1700hrs to "make the line more secure and determine the enemy position and strength." He specifically insisted that the patrols go "as far as they can go." Delays in the transmission of the orders resulted in the patrols not getting started until 1830hrs. Despite difficulty in picking their way through the woods in the gathering darkness, the Marines occupied the Bois de Halibat and the Bois de Montagne without resistance.

To the east the 5th Division was also ordered to dispatch strong patrols. After delays in coordinating sufficient artillery support, the 3/6th and 1/11th moved forward at 1700hrs. The Germans responded with artillery and moved into Bonvaux, and the 1/11th secured the Bois Hanido. The 3/6th continued their advance despite German defensive fire and secured outposts north of Bonvaux by 2000hrs. Contact was established with the Marines at Rembercourt and the attack was suspended. The offensive was over.

AFTERMATH

By the end of September 13, First Army had captured 16,000 Germans, killed or wounded as many or more, and captured 450 artillery pieces. Total American casualties were roughly 7,000 killed and wounded.

It was not until late on September 14 that the scales fell from the eyes of First Army headquarters. Although the night march of the 102nd Regiment had closed off the German line of retreat, it had come too late. Nearly 40,000 Germans had escaped from the salient.

The II Colonial Corps failed to actively engage the Germans in the nose of the salient and by doing so delay their withdrawal. The French offensive was unenthusiastic and their attacks haphazard. Once the Mihiel Group began to retreat the French did nothing to pursue them.

Clausewitz wrote that the essential characteristics of offensive warfare were decision, speed, and continuity of effort. Evaluated against that standard the American effort fell short. Pershing and his staff had developed a credible plan but with limited objectives. The tentative nature of those objectives reflected the expectation of determined resistance from the enemy coupled

American officers examining a captured German 210mm howitzer.

The American cemetery at Thiaucourt soon after its opening in the 1920s. The cemetery, occupying 40 acres, contains the graves of 4,153 American dead, including 177 "unknowns."

with the knowledge that the timetable for the Meuse–Argonne offensive required the withdrawal of key divisions during the second day of the attack.

The first 48 hours were the key to potential American success at St Mihiel. Although provisional orders issued during the morning of September 12 attempted to respond to the rapidly shifting situation, in which American units were quickly outpacing the schedule and overrunning their objectives, there were inevitable delays and confusion.

In the first 24 hours the Americans' failure to effect the juncture of the 26th and 1st divisions at Vigneulles allowed the majority of the Germans at the nose of the salient to escape. Dickman charged that if the 1st Division had displayed "energy and skill in night marching" the Vigneulles–St Benoît road would have been cut four to six hours earlier, trapping the bulk of the Combres Group as it retreated. Despite their dramatic night march on September 12–13 the failure of the 26th Division to deploy adequate reserves in a timely manner in the late morning of September 12 delayed their eventual march to Vigneulles.

Even after failing to trap the bulk of the retreating Germans, the Americans had an opportunity to exploit German disorganization. A renewed American attack could have breached the Michel Stellung but in order to fully exploit a breakthrough substantial resources would have needed to be committed, which was impossible with the timetable for the Meuse–Argonne offensive overshadowing any future plans. During the second 24 hours a lack of aggressive movements or any attacks on the Michel Stellung missed the opportunity to punch a hole in it.

The First Army intelligence briefing issued on September 12 concluded that the enemy had begun their withdrawal and that the Germans intended to make a stand at the Michel Stellung. The report also suggested that although the Germans could "make a stiff resistance on the Hindenburg Line tomorrow, he will be numerically much inferior to us for several days yet."

Although they had stemmed the American advance and avoided the loss of the bulk of their infantry, the German high command viewed St Mihiel as a major defeat. On September 13, Hindenburg questioned Gallwitz on the deployment of the reserve divisions and the hasty withdrawal of Army Detachment C. On September 17, with the threat of further American advances still a real possibility, Hindenburg told Gallwitz that "the severe defeat of Army Detachment C on September 12 has rendered the situation of the Group of Armies critical … caused by the most part by faulty leadership … the Group of Armies will bear the responsibility for this."

The success of the St Mihiel offensive was a vindication of Pershing's long and seemingly intractable struggles with both the French and English to establish a separate identity for the First US Army. The significance of the St Mihiel offensive was not in the actual battle as it was fought, but that it demonstrated that, despite the skepticism of both the British and French leadership, the Americans could undertake large-scale offensive operations. Through that demonstration the issue of amalgamation was finally put to rest. Fox Conner contended that, "The greatest result of the operation was the development of the First Army as an effective offensive weapon for more vital fighting." In addition to proving command competence, St Mihiel also witnessed the establishment of American airpower and armored forces and the emergence of future military leaders such as Patton, MacArthur, and Mitchell.

While the focus of attention shifted northward to the Meuse–Argonne the St Mihiel front remained something of a sideshow. Although evidence increased daily that the Americans were massing troops in the Meuse–Argonne region, Gallwitz continued to be plagued by suspicions that Pershing might be staging an elaborate ruse in order to draw German reserves away from the Michel Stellung.

In order to keep the German high command off balance, American forces along the Michel Stellung continued aggressive patrolling and launched several high-profile raids. On September 25 American forces along the Michel Stellung launched a series of raids designed to focus German attention away from the Meuse–Argonne. The American IV Corps, now composed of the 78th, 90th, 89th, and 42nd divisions, engaged in a series of attacks along their fronts. The 42nd organized a raid on Marchéville and found itself locked in a desperate running battle that ended with over 300 men dead, wounded, or missing.

After a short halt to reorganize, the First US Army resumed the Meuse–Argonne offensive on November 1. American forces broke through the German lines west of the Meuse River, resulting in a wholesale German retreat. On November 5 Pershing turned his attention back to the St Mihiel sector, ordering the Second US Army to begin preparation for a general offensive to capture Briey.

The Second US Army launched a general attack on November 9, with mixed results. Foch upped the ante, proposing to expand the offensive to include a French army group to the south and the First US Army to the north. In preparation for this new attack, American divisions fought and doughboys died right up until the final armistice at 1100hrs on November 11, 1918.

THE BATTLEFIELD TODAY

The St Mihiel battlefield remains much as it was in 1918. The region's landscape is still characterized by rolling hills, interspersed with woodlands and small towns. The remains of German fortifications can be found throughout the region.

There are two American memorials in the area. The St Mihiel American Cemetery is located west of Thiaucourt. In its approximately 40 acres are buried 4,153 American dead. At the center of the cemetery is a large sundial surmounted by an American eagle. The site also includes a statue of a World War I soldier and a white stone memorial consisting of a small chapel and a map building. The chapel contains a mosaic portraying an angel sheathing his sword and on two walls of the museum are recorded the names of 284 of the missing.

The Montsec American Monument is located on the hill of Montsec, 12 miles southeast of the St Mihiel American Cemetery. The monument is dedicated to the American offensive and consists of a large circular colonnade, at the center of which, on a raised platform, is a bronze relief map of the St Mihiel salient. Around the top of the colonnade are the names of the towns captured by the Americans during the offensive. Along the stair leading to the colonnade is an engraved dedication reading:

This Monument has been erected by the United States of America to commemorate the capture of the St Mihiel salient by the troops of her first army and to record the services of the American Expeditionary forces on the battlefields in this region and elsewhere in Lorraine and in Alsace. It stands as a lasting symbol of the friendship and cooperation between the French and American armies.

LEFT
The American cemetery at Thiaucourt, shown in the 1920s.

RIGHT
The American monument at Montsec.

BIBLIOGRAPHY

Asprey, Robert B., *The German High Command at War*, William Morrow: New York, 1991

Benwell, Harry A., *History of the Yankee Division*, Cornhill: Boston, MA, 1919

Blumenson, Martin, *The Patton Papers, 1885–1940*, Houghton Mifflin: Boston, 1972

Brannen, Carl Andrew, *Over There, A Marine in the Great War*, Texas A&M Press: College Station, 1996

Brown, William and Tuttle, Birdeena, *The Adventures of an American Doughboy*, Smith-Kinney: Tacoma, WA, 1919

Bullard, Robert L., *Personalities and Reminiscences of the War*, Doubleday: New York, 1925

Clark, George B., *Devil Dogs*, Presidio Press: Novato, CA, 1999

Coffman, Edward, *The War to End All Wars*, University of Wisconsin Press: Madison, WI, 1986

Eisenhower, John S. D., *Yanks*, Free Press: New York, 2001

English, George H., *History of the 89th Division*, War Society of the 89th Division: 1920

Farwell, Byron, *Over There*, W. W. Norton: New York, 1999

German Army Handbook, 1918, Hippocrene Books: New York, 1977

Gowenlock, Thomas, *Soldiers of Darkness*, Doubleday, Doran and Company: New York, 1937

Grotelueschen, Mark Ethan, *The AEF Way of War*, Cambridge University Press: Cambridge, MA, 2007

Hallas, James H., *Squandered Victory*, Praeger: Westport, CT, 1995

Hamilton, Craig, *Echoes from Over There*, Soldiers' Publishing Company: New York, 1919

Harries, Meirion and Susie, *The Last Days of Innocence*, Random House: New York, 1997

History of the 90th Division, Ninetieth Division Association: 1920

Hudson, James J., *Hostile Skies*, Syracuse University Press: Syracuse, New York, 1968

Krass, Peter, *Portrait of War*, Wiley and Sons: Hoboken, NJ, 2007

Liggett, Hunter, *Commanding an American Army*, Houghton Mifflin: Boston, 1925

Marshall, George C., *Memoirs of My Service in the World War, 1917–1918*, Houghton Mifflin: Boston, 1976

Masseck, C. J., *Brief History of the 89th Division*, US Government Printing Office: Washington, DC, 1919

Mosier, John, *Myth of the Great War*, Harper Collins: New York, 2001

Order of Battle of the United States Land Forces in the World War, US Government Printing Office: Washington, DC, 1931

Owen, Peter F., *To the Limits of Endurance, A Battalion of Marines in the Great War*, Texas A&M Press: College Station, TX, 2007

Pershing, John J., *Final Report of General John J. Pershing, Commander in Chief American Expeditionary Forces*, Washington Printing Office: Washington, DC, 1920

Pershing, John J., *My Experiences in the World War*, Frederick Stokes: New York, 1931

Strickland, Daniel W., *Connecticut Fights*, Quinnipiack Press: New Haven, CT, 1930

Second Division AEF, 1917–1919, Battery Press: Nashville, TN, 1989

Sibley, Frank P., *With the Yankee Division in France*, Little Brown: 1919

Thompson, Hugh S., *Trench Knives and Mustard Gas, With the 42nd Rainbow Division in France*, Texas A&M University Press: College Station, TX, 2004

Trask, David F., *The AEF and Coalition Warmaking 1917–1918*, University Press of Kansas: Lawrence, KS, 1993

Viereck, G. S., *As They Saw Us*, Doubleday: New York, 1929

Wilson, Dale E., *Treat 'Em Rough*, Presidio Press: Novato, CA, 1989

Wright, William M., *Meuse–Argonne Diary*, University of Missouri Press: Columbia, MO, 2004

INDEX

Numbers in **bold** refer to plates, maps and illustrations.